DATE DUE

DEMCO 38-296

SPALDING.

Field Hockey

W.F. Axton
and
Wendy Lee Martin

MP
MASTERS PRESS

A Division of Howard W. Sams & Co.

Published by Masters Press
(A Division of Howard W. Sams & Co.)
2647 Waterfront Pkwy. E. Dr., Suite 300
Indianapolis, IN 46214

Library of Congress Cataloging-in-Publication Data

Axton, William F.

    Field Hockey / W.F. Axton and Wendy Lee Martin.
         p.   cm. — (Spalding sports library)
    At head of title: Spalding.
    ISBN 0-940279-81-9
    1. Field Hockey. I. Martin, Wendy Lee, 1954 — . II. Title.
III. Title: Spalding field hockey. IV. Series.
GV1017.H7A98   1993   93-33063
796.355--dc20   CIP

10 9 8 7 6 5 4 3

TABLE OF CONTENTS

Credits:

Interior photos by Anne M. Axton

Models: Samantha Axton, Sara Butorac, Chase Keith, and Jeannie Gentile

Front cover photo by Mark Lynch provided by the University of Louisville Sports Information Department

Back cover photo provided by the University of Connecticut Sports Information Department.

Cover design by Lynne Annette Clark

Text design by Leah Marckel

Edited by Holly Witten Kondras

Preface

At an awards banquet for the girls' field hockey team of the Louisville Collegiate School in November, 1990, a wise and witty parent of the Most Valuable Player referred to the championship game, which had exhausted every possible tie-breaking procedure in the rulebook before at long last it produced a winner. He concluded, "Never have I agonized so much over a game about which I know so little." That pregnant comment yields a generalization about field hockey: "Never on the field of play has there ever been a game about which so many have agonized so much while knowing so little."

This introduction to field hockey is designed to remedy that pervasive state of ignorance about the game felt among beginning players afield and spectators along the sidelines. Its authors are, first, a successful (200 + wins) and knowledgeable coach on the secondary level, a master of the technics and mystique of the sport, and, second, the father of two daughters who have played varsity field hockey before his all-uncomprehending eyes for a dozen years or more. It was past time, he concluded, to learn enough about the game to follow it with some understanding of what was going on afield. Finding no volume that addressed his ignorance, he turned to his daughters' coach for help; and between them they have put together this guide. In what follows, be assured, the substance is hers, and the form (and mistakes) his. We hope it will be of use to novice players and coaches as well as to spectators.

It is a rare book that is the product of a single, unassisted, mind, and this work is no exception. At the outset, let us acknowledge the invaluable assistance of the doyenne of field hockey in Kentucky, Coach "Bunny" Daugherty, herself a historian of the game and veritable encyclopedia of its past in the Bluegrass State, whose generosity, kindness, and grasp of the game are legendary. Without her, this little volume would be the poorer.

A number of patient and helpful people have read this manuscript at various stages of its writing and offered useful comment, notably Michael Hardesty, field hockey columnist, fount of information, and devotee of the game; Martha Neal Cooke, who knows what books ought to be; Penelope Morton, quondam player and shrewd observer, who has a keen eye for the proper order of things, and Anne Axton, parental veteran of the field hockey wars whose imprimitur is not easily gained.

Let us also give thanks to all those parents who helped us in this mighty work, if only by inquiring, some time or other, "What the devil did she do THAT for?" or "Why am I cheering NOW?" At last, we hope, they'll know.

Field Hockey

Introduction
Deciding to Play:
What's Involved

Since field hockey is only a game, after all, the decision about playing or not playing should be left up to the young person. It goes without saying that a decision to participate in a sport, all things being equal, is not a decision an adult makes for a child nor is it one that should be coerced. Parents who push their children into such activities without the child's wholehearted dedication to them are exploiting their children for their own vicarious gratification.

It follows, therefore, that the reason to play a sport like field hockey is that it is fun — fun for the players to play and fun for parents, friends, and fans to watch. When playing ceases to be fun it's time to quit. We don't mean to imply that every moment of a participant's time in hockey will be transfigured with ecstatic joy. On the contrary, to be good in any sport requires the same kind of hard work and repetitious practice which is required in much of a student's classroom work. The fun part comes when hard, slogging work pays off in skillful performance, in a winning shot on goal or a flawless defensive tackle or stop. There's a special thrill in being part of a team when it "clicks," when everything goes right, the game comes together, and the team plays well as a unit. Then players feel proud of themselves and their teammates, and those who love them are proud of them too. The players have set a goal for themselves, they've worked hard to prepare, and now they've succeeded. When well played, as they discover, field hockey is an endlessly fascinating game.

Sometimes, in spite of all of a person's best efforts, she fails. Learning how to come to terms with failure is one of the most useful lessons a young person can learn, particularly in a society such as ours, which doesn't like to think about not succeeding. Learning how to handle victory is easy; how to handle defeat is difficult. Everyone needs help.

Needing help is where team sports like field hockey come in. Teammates, if they're good teammates, offer comfort when things go wrong. They're also there to cheer a player when she finally gets it right, and she will reciprocate. More importantly, teammates are colleagues in a common enterprise, the team, and each will draw strength from that cooperative association. Team play requires that each participant relate to the other players on her team in the interest of the success of the team as a whole. Teamwork is another word for cooperation, in which the immediate aims of the individual are subordinated to the efficient execution of a coordinated group exercise. At the same time, it asks for the best of individual achievement as well. All that mutual interlinking of helping and being helped works like a geodesic dome: it makes a structure that seems insubstantial but resists the stresses of adversity. One reason we are so interested in competitive team sports is that they teach us, in a game situation, how life itself should be played: with rules, and by the rules, recognizing that we're all in this thing together.

People who play an organized team sport, generally speaking, take better care of themselves than those who don't. Nicotine, alcohol, and other toxic substances have no place in the life of anyone playing a team sport, where stamina, speed, coordination and physical fitness are essential attributes of participants. Varsity athletes are likely to be careful about what and how much they eat, about rest and healthy relaxation, and about leading disciplined lives.

Field hockey is not a game that is especially hard on the body, and injuries are few and not usually serious. Because players carry sticks, the rules governing play and the way players are coached stress avoidance of dangerous actions like high backswings and follow-throughs and hard-hit high balls. Penalties for dangerous play are severe. Mouth guards and shin guards offer protection, but knuckles will be struck by sticks and hard-hit balls are going to bang into thighs and bodies. They will hurt enough to make players cry sometimes and will leave some spectacularly colorful bruises. Sprained ankles are not uncommon, as is stress on the knees — about what a person might expect from a game with so much running in it.

Field hockey is also not especially hard on the academics, either. The usual season runs about two months in the autumn, plus three weeks or so of pre-season practice. Counting a league tournament early in November, there may be twenty games in all — two a week on average. Practice sessions last an hour and a half or two hours after school in the afternoon, but rarely on weekends. Spring practices are not usual, though selected players in the USFHA "Futures" program may put in a weekend a month during the winter and spring and perhaps a week all told in summer tournament play. For other players, week-long summer hockey camps are available in different parts of the country.

Nor is field hockey hard on the budget, either an individual's or their school's. Except for the goalkeeper, whose gear can run into the hundreds of dollars, equipment and uniforms are simple and inexpensive. Schools need to provide a field to play on and the maintenance to keep it fit for competition, a couple of goal cages, tables for the officials, benches for the teams, and, to complete the ensemble, that insignificant trifle the coach, who doubles as a PE instructor.

Since getting an education is more important than playing a sport, it doesn't make sense to allow one's choice of a school to hinge on its field hockey program. Nor should a student with borderline grades think about playing any sport until those marks are acceptable–"C" or better. Good schools won't permit it, anyway. Holding out the prospect of participating in a sport when grades improve can be a splendid motivator for hitting the books, providing it's understood that staying with the sport involves staying with the books, too. In many cases, borderline grades improve when students participate in a sport, since, knowing they must perform well in the classroom, they are forced to better organize their time. Then too, making the team is a great builder of self esteem, which often shows up off the field as well as on it.

If games were left entirely to children and young people, except for trained officials and coaches who are also teachers, varsity sports might have fewer unpleasant side effects than they do. But some schools, school systems and administrators, journalists, parents and others have laden a few varsity sports with an elaborate paraphernalia of hype that has little to do with sport, fun, growing up, or education. In most places, we're happy to say, field hockey has escaped the biggest part of all that hoopla and flapdoodle: there's no big pay-off in the pros to poison the well.

No thoughtful parent will allow a child who participates in a sport to be unduly pressured merely for the sake of winning a game, making the varsity, being voted MVP, getting a college scholarship, or whatever. Young people are passionate about their commitments and allegiances, and have no need of further emotional exploitation. All by themselves they can get so wound up about their playtime activities as to lose sleep before a game or to come down with the fantods if they play poorly or lose. It is therefore highly counter-productive for the adults around them to reinforce these intense feelings with their own quite inexcusable hysterics. Grown-ups are supposed to be there to offer support, solace, and – most of all – perspective, and to be role-models of mature behavior in the stands and at home. Elsewhere in these pages we speak explicitly about spectatorial deportment. Here we simply enjoin that parents try not to be one of those infamous "Little-League Moms and Pops" immortalized in song and story.

Having said that, let's get on with hockey. "The game's afoot, Watson!" as Holmes would cry.

Chapter One
History and Organization

Field Hockey played by girls and young women, the game known to Americans, was part of that great movement of the last century and a half which we now refer to, rather grandly, as the physical emancipation of women. Tennis and golf are other sports to which women gravitated during the later years of the nineteenth century and the earlier years of the twentieth, supplanting the more decorous activities previously thought proper for the "weaker sex," such as croquet, ballroom dancing, cards, billiards, visiting, music, walking, and botanizing.

This growth of active sports for women was but one manifestation of a much more extensive movement toward involvement by all sorts of people in more or less strenuous physical activity on some kind of grassy playing field in the out-of-doors. Baseball, cricket, soccer, football, track-and-field, and the like, all had their period of greatest development when Victoria sat upon the British throne. Then it was that a mass audience of sports enthusiasts came into being, the word fanatic was shortened to fan, and a whole industry catering to the sports-minded was created.

A great many causative factors had to come together to make this revolution in leisure activity take place: A society wealthy enough to have time to kill. A society which values competition. A sedentary urban society that wants and needs exercise for play. A society with the technology to create surfaces smooth enough so that these games afield can be played with skill and precision. (We forget that the reel lawnmower and the lawn roller, inventions of the middle years of the nineteenth century, made possible a high level of skill in field sports and in this way contributed to their popularity. Sheep and scythes just couldn't do the job.)

Originated in India, field hockey was brought to England in the middle years of the nineteenth century, where it soon became the national sport for women. By 1886, the English Hockey Association had been formed, and the modern game defined by the adoption of the striking circle (see Chapter Two). Europeans took up the game not long after, and there, as in the rest of the world where it's played, it remains a popular sport of both sexes. The United States is unique in that here field hockey is largely a women's sport. Even so, the U.S. men's field hockey team has played in the Olympics since 1932 and the women's team since 1980. It is one of the few truly amateur international team sports.

Field hockey came to the United States in 1901, when an irrepressible 28-year-old Englishwoman, Constance M.K. Applebee, a member of the British College of Physical Education, introduced the game to a group of participants in a summer sports symposium at Harvard University, laying out the field with chalk in a small concrete yard beside the gym and using ice hockey sticks and an indoor baseball. Vassar College invited Miss Applebee to teach the game to its students the same year, and it was an instant success. She soon introduced the young women of Smith, Mt. Holyoke, Radcliffe, Wellesley, and Bryn Mawr to field hockey, and eventually settled down to a faculty appointment at the latter institution.

A single-minded person, Miss Applebee immediately began organizing women's and girl's field hockey clubs in the Philadelphia area, which still has the biggest concentration of them in the country; by 1922 she had established a sports camp in the Pocono Mountains for field hockey coaches and players where she taught for the next 43 summers. In the same year she was instru- mental in organizing the United States Field Hockey Association (USFHA), which remains the sport's governing body in this country; and for many years thereafter she was its presiding genius. It is safe to say that American women's field hockey is the creation of this long-lived and determined woman.

About 14,000 serious women players today are members of the USFHA, subscribe to its house-organ, the *Eagle*, and participate in its various activities like the "Futures" program. Its male equivalent is the Field Hockey Association of America, with about 1,100 members. Nationally, the USFHA comprises nine geographical regions where field hockey is played: Great Lakes, Midwest, Mid-East, New Atlantic, Northeast, Pacific Northwest, Pacific Southwest, Phil- adelphia, and Southeast.

Until April 1993, field hockey in the United States was governed by two separate organiations, the USFHA for women and the Field Hockey Associ- ation of America (FHAA) for men. Because the U.S. Olympic Committe would no longer recognize two organizations governing one sport, the USFA applied for and was granted the status of the National Governing Body for field hockey in the United States.

There is also only one governing body for both international men and women's field hockey, the Federation Internationale de Hockey located in Brussels, Belgium.

The USFHA encourages junior programs for beginning teams, usually starting in the fourth or fifth grades, and will lend equipment packages for them, and assistance in finding or training coaches and officials, anywhere in the country, providing an adult or an institution – a school or club, say – is willing to sponsor the group. By the same token, USFHA-sanctioned regional summer camps for secondary-school players, coaches and game officials offer opportunities to improve competitive skills and meet new people. The USFHA "Futures" program, designed to develop a national pool of highly skilled teen-aged players on both the middle- and upper school levels, includes weekend practices at indoor facilities during the winter, regional invitational tournaments in late spring, and national invitational tournaments among teams of regional all-stars in high summer. Outstanding players are identified and invited to attend a sequence of advanced training camps – "C," "B," and "A," in that order. Many college coaches attend these tournaments as spectators, others as coaches. The aim is to make the United States internationally competitive in womens' field hockey.

Field hockey is played by girls in middle school and high school and by young women in college and beyond, on teams representing private and parochial schools as well as public institutions, universities, and clubs. About 1200 secondary schools and over 325 colleges and universities in the United States field teams on every level of play, from Big Ten, ACC, and Ivy League powerhouses to small liberal arts colleges with 1000 students or less. Many also maintain intramural field hockey leagues for dorm and house teams. Some schools award athletic scholarships in field hockey, and participation in the game on a varsity level in secondary school is one of those activities that collegiate admission officers like to see, even if athletic scholarships are not offered, especially if the player is good and indicates that she may want to play on the NCAA level. In any autumn season, more than 50,000 women and girls, and upwards of 7,500 men and boys, are actively engaged in playing the game on organized teams in the United States. Hundreds of thousands of women have been players in youth and/or follow the sport in afterlife as members of club teams or as spectators. If a person is in reasonably good shape – she runs or jogs a couple of miles three or four times a week – she can enjoy a weekend of club hockey for a long time to come. Some club teams are downright serious about the game, and all like the sociability fostered by team sports.

Participation in field hockey at all levels is growing as new teams are organized in communities heretofore without access to this fascinating game, and established leagues find newly organized teams springing up hither and yon. Since the 1970s women's field hockey has been one of the chief beneficiaries of the equal rights movement in the United States as that has been applied to inter-collegiate and intra-mural athletics. Its future as a major women's varsity sport seems assured. Even so, at this writing field hockey teams are not evenly distributed among the states. Outside of New England and the Mid-Atlantic states, where the sport is to be found everywhere, field hockey is likely to be concentrated in the larger urban and suburban areas. Field hockey clubs are everywhere, often in unlikely places.

For more information, contact:

United States Field Hockey Association
1750 Boulder Street
Colorado Springs, CO 80909-5773
(719) 578-4567

Annual rulebooks for school field hockey may be ordered from:

National Federation of State High School Associations
11724 Plaza Circle
P.O. Box 20626
Kansas City, MO 64195
(816) 464-5400

In Canada contact:

Field Hockey Canada
802-1600 Promenade
James Naismith Drive
Gloucester, Ontario T1B 5N4
CANADA
(613) 748-5634

Chapter Two
The Playing Field

Field hockey is played on a field 100 yards long and 60 yards wide (see diagram) by two teams of 11 players equipped with sticks that have a curved end or "toe" used to strike a ball. The teams occupy opposite ends of the field, and change ends to start the second half. The object of the game is to put the ball into the opponents' goal – a net or cage 12 feet wide, seven feet high, and four feet deep at ground level – at the other end of the field. Each goal made scores a point.

High-schoolers play two 30 minute halves with a 10-minute intermission. For middle-school players, it's 25 minute halves, for collegians it's 35 minute halves and five-minute intermission. Substitutions are permitted when play is stopped by a foul call and penalty – usually a free hit – or a side-in (when the ball is returned to play after being hit out of bounds) except during the last five minutes of the game. (To be perfectly technical, substitutions are permitted only when your own team has the ball on a penalty, but if the other team is substituting during their free hit, then one's own subs may enter as well.) One time-out of 60 seconds is allowed in each half for each team, except under NCAA rules; an official may call a time-out to tend to an injured player or in case of taxing weather conditions. You will know when the game is nearing its end because the time-keeper stands up on the sidelines. There are some complicated procedures for tie-breakers that we'll get into later.

The circle of five yards radius at midfield marks the place where play commences at the start of the first half and the second half and after goals have been scored. A pre-game coin toss determines which team will begin play; the other team then starts the second half. The team just scored upon gets to put the ball in play from the midfield circle. Play is begun by a pass-back: that is, the teams line up across the field facing each other and no closer than five yards to the ball, and a player from the appropriate team hits, pushes, or lofts the ball back to a teammate. (Under NCAA rules, lofting is forbidden.)

Before anything else you need to know that the outside edge of the end and the side lines mark the boundary of the playing field. A ball is not out of bounds until all of it is entirely over the line, rather than on it. The goal, therefore, is set on the outside edge of the end line. When the entire ball has been hit completely over that line by an attacker, a goal has been scored. To paraphrase Yogi Berra, in field hockey a ball ain't out till the whole ball is out. Similarly, it ain't in (the goal) till it's completely in.

The first thing that a person may notice is that the field of play is divided into quarters, not ones, fives, and tens of yards, as in football, the reason being that field hockey, like soccer and rugby, is a game of continuous movement and not, like American football, one of a succession of set plays designed to gain territory, achieve position, and control an area.

Another peculiarity is that half-circle 16 yards in radius in front of each goal cage, called the striking circle. In school hockey, only goals hit into the cage from within this half-circle can be counted. Goals hit from outside are invalid unless the ball hits the stick of an attacking player inside the striking circle. In NCAA hockey, however, a goal can be scored from anywhere inside the 25-yard line, not just from the striking circle. That change opens up the game and makes it much more rapid and fluid. It also means that balls come whistling in toward the goal. In addition, fouls committed inside the striking circle are treated differently from those elsewhere on the field, where the usual penalty is a free hit by the other team taken at the spot of the infraction.

Suffice it to say, the line marking the striking circle is the most important line on the field. It is drawn as two arcs each having the apex at a front corner of the goal cage, except that the four yards opposite the open mouth of the cage is a straight line parallel to the end line. The striking circle is thus not really a half circle inscribed from one side of the end line to the other: instead it is two arcs linked by a straight line four yards long exactly 16 yards upfield from the goal. There is a hashmark on each side line at the 16-yard point, to indicate the place where the 16-yard hit may be taken by the defenders after a turnover.

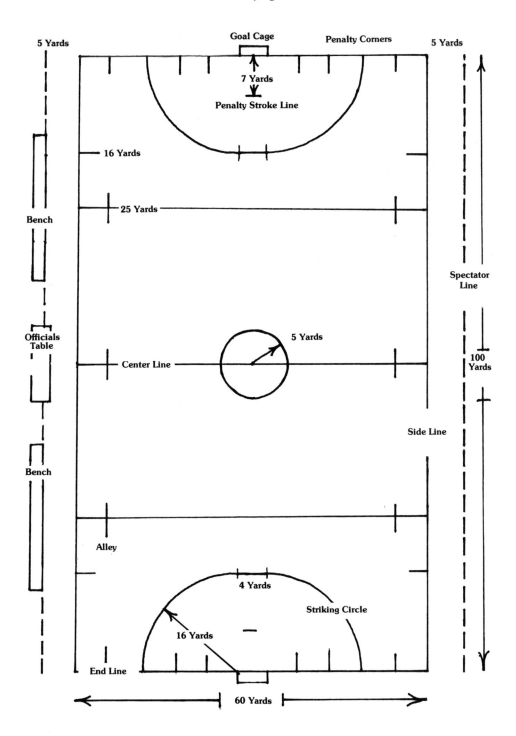

The field of play

Inside the striking circle and seven yards in front of the goal cage is a line a foot long. This is the penalty stroke line, from which an attacking player, in a penalty or an overtime tie-breaker situation, goes face-to-face against the goalkeeper for a possible score.

On the end line, ten yards on either side of the goal cage, are hashmarks called the penalty corner lines where the ball is placed in play by the attacking team when the defense has fouled inside the striking circle. The two hashmarks five yards from either end of the goal cage mark the outer limits of the place where the defensive players may station themselves in a penalty corner situation. They can't be closer than five yards to the attackers. Farther out on the end line is a hashmark five yards in from the side line, to mark the Wings' alley down the side line. It is also the place where the long hit is taken by the offense after a defensive turnover inside the circle. About the corner shot, the penalty line, the long hit and the 16-yard hit, more later: they're part of the intricacies of this game.

The officials' table and, on either side of that, the team benches are handled as they are in basketball — they're all on one side of the field, and at least five yards away from the sideline, the same distance as that separating the spectators from the playing field on the other side. Players need that space for side-ins — putting the ball back in play after it goes out-of-bounds. Spectators are enjoined to stay away from the end line and to avoid abusing, advising, or trying to engage the goalkeeper in conversation during the game. Persistent violators of this rule may be asked by the referee to leave the premises or be otherwise disciplined.

There are, by the way, two referees, one for each side of the field, suitably attired in a black-and-white striped shirt and equipped with a whistle and some penalty cards. Each official is responsible for policing the action inside his or her side of a diagonal line drawn between opposite corners of the field: from the far corner on the right to the near corner on the left. Each has a goal to superintend, together with the playing field at that end. A scorer and a timer at the officials' table preside over the scorebook and the clock and stopwatch, respectively.

A final word about the field itself. For field hockey to be played as it should be, an artificial surface is desirable, and seven-a-side winter hockey indoors requires it absolutely. Even so, an Astroturf football field with its extreme drainage curvature is not the optimum field hockey surface since the fall of the surface makes accurate passing difficult. Field hockey is a passing game, and the ideal field ought to approximate a level golf green. The ball should roll, not bounce — ever. A field on which football, soccer, or lacrosse are regularly played is much too rough for a rational game of hockey.

If a level artificial surface is not to be had, the next best thing is a grass field. Many authorities would argue that a natural grass field, properly designed and maintained, is preferable to any alternative, and point to shining examples. A lawn of tough, deep-rooted grass trimmed to an inch or an inch and a half and regularly leveled, resodded and reseeded, top-dressed, watered, fertilized, and rolled can make a superb playing surface. But no other sport should be played on the field, to avoid cutting it up.

It's not too much to say that the character of the playing surface determines the level of play possible in this game — just as it does in baseball or billiards.

Chapter Three
The Players: Gear

We've seen that a field hockey team consists of 11 players on a side. Before we go any further we should spend a minute on their equipment. All the players but the goal keeper use the same gear, and it's simple gear at that.

STICKS

Every player has the same basic kind of stick, usually made of ash or mulberry wood for more or less flexibility, between 35 and 38 inches in length and weighing between 18 and 23 ounces. (Knock off an inch and an ounce for junior – middle school or younger – players). It may be wrapped with some material and have a rubber, towel, or suede grip. Sticks differ in their distribution of weight, however, some having weight added in the toe, others with a more balanced heft. Individual preference is the rule here: get what feels most comfortable. In choosing a stick, a player should grab it with both hands near the top (left hand highest) with the arms hanging comfortably straight down in front of the body. The swing should make the club's curved toe sweep the top of the grass (or thick-pile rug) in front of the feet and not touch the ground. The best weight may be determined by holding the stick in the left hand and controlling it one handedly while swinging it. If a player can readily control the stick with the left hand, it's the right one. But take note: if a player stays with field hockey very long, she'll probably be growing taller, and her original stick will almost certainly suffer the slings and arrows of outrageous fortune – that is, it will get beat-up – so a player is likely to have to get another stick or two along the way, just to keep her keen competitive edge.

Notice that the curved toe of the stick is flat on one side, rounded on the other — the reason for that asymmetry being that only the flat side – that's the left hand side as the player holds the stick before her – may legally hit the ball. Hitting a backhand therefore requires that the stick be reversed a half-circle

(180-degrees) to the left in a counter-clockwise direction — one of the fiendish subtleties of this game, which is prone to perverse rules. (There are no sticks for lefthanders.) Because of this asymmetry, hockey has a distinctly right-to-left bias, with many implications for the way the game is played.

SHOES

Low-cut turf shoes or soccer cleats (rubber or plastic) are best on grass. On artificial surfaces turf shoes are preferred, unless it's wet; then tennis shoes should be worn. Sorry! No metal spikes, cleats, or studs allowed.

SHIN GUARDS

Field hockey is, after all, played with sticks, so guards for the fore parts of lower legs are definitely in order, either stuffed in long socks or held in place by straps that buckle behind the calf. They may be made of plastic, fiberglass, or rubber.

LONG SOCKS

In one of the team's colors, to hold shin guards and to help officials distinguish between the teams when making close calls in a melee of legs and sticks.

MOUTH GUARDS

Plastic mouth guards that can be softened to fit a player's teeth (molars included) are required, to cut her losses in case she walks into a wild stick or a high cannon-shot.

BALLS

Most balls nowadays are plastic, white or any other color (including fluorescent orange or yellow for night games), and can be purchased at the local sports emporium. However put together, they must weigh 5 ½ to 5 ¾ ounces and measure 8 ¾ to 9 ¼ inches around. Players will probably need two or three balls for practice at home, one to lose, and one for the dog to eat. If she has a little brother, she'll need even more.

UNIFORMS

The rulebook is pretty loose about attire, except that blouses be numbered (1 to 99) front (2″ to 4″) and back (4″ to 6″), the home team's light in color and the visitors' dark. The same color differences apply to high socks/sock guards, which also must be worn. No jewelry, of course, and only soft hair-control devices like scarves or sweatbands. Sweatpants, tights, gloves, and even knitted hats may be worn, as appropriate for the weather and playing conditions. Again, they must observe the home-away distinction in color. A player in an illegal uniform, however, shall be removed from the game WITHOUT SUBSTITUTION at the first stoppage of play, and may return to action, when dressed properly, only at the next interruption of play. Hard sayings!

GOAL-KEEPERS (GOALIES)

Goalies are, by way of gear, a thing apart, for their position in the eye of the storm, so to speak, requires special protection from multitudes of sticks and balls, and they are loaded down with equipment. Starting at the top, a Goalie must wear a Jason mask or (preferably) a wire basket mask and football-like helmet. Below that a foam rubber neck protector, then a chest protector that resembles a bullet-proof vest, then a padded apron for the pelvis, thigh pads, and from the knees down goalie leg pads like those used in ice hockey, and special square-toed goalie kickers that fasten over the shoes. On her hands she wears heavily padded goalie's gloves, and for reasons that will become obvious hereafter, she carries her stick, gripped in the middle, in her right hand. A jersey of the right color must be worn over the chest protector. The wide leg pads impart to the goalie's stride an ominous stomping motion that observers associate with dinosaurs closing in on their helpless prey.

The parents of a goalie will want to provide her, in addition to a lot of emotional support, with a big canvas seabag or the equivalent in which to carry all her gear. Attention, goalie mothers: keeping her equipment smelling tolerable is an ongoing operation. Good luck. The other players travel light: for them a draw-string ditty-bag will do. There's a long narrow bag with a sling to go over the shoulder for carrying multiple sticks in that some players affect, even though field hockey is not at all like golf. It serves no discernable purpose. It is, however, powerfully impressive in hanging around airport lobbies with. Coupled with a level gaze and a mouth set just so, a stick bag can create such an intense effect of cool as to frost the most jaded sophisticate and cause players on the other team to dissolve into dead alien goo. It softens airline flight attendants, too. Players should prevail upon indulgent parents to get them one.

One other piece of equipment is the Ace bandage, well nigh obligatory wear for the field hockey player who wishes to convey to onlookers that, if they only knew, she is a veteran of the field hockey wars, bears innumerable scars, and can play hurt with the best of them. Since only about one Ace bandage in a hundred has any benefit other than that of moral adornment, we put it here, under equipment. If your orthopedic surgeon prescribes it, then wear it, silly, and tell scoffers to bug off. In all cases, the Ace bandage should be as grungy as possible — one-upmanship, you know.

A final note: before the game you'll see the referees checking out the players, who have lined up. That's to make sure everyone is properly dressed and equipped and to correlate players with rosters. Earlier they will have gone over the field, explained any pertinent ground rules, introduced the rival captains, and tossed the coin for choice of goal or opening possession of the ball. Sometimes they may ask what the Ace bandage is for. Have an answer ready.

Chapter Four
The Players: Positions

As we shall soon see, field hockey has its own vocabulary, full of slang words and technical terms that make outsiders feel like strangers in a strange land. Nowhere is this confusion of tongues more noticeable than in the names given to various positions on the team, which differ from coach to coach according to the formations used and the style of play. But then, that is true of many sports, isn't it? Think of football's five-twos and four-threes and wide-tackle sixes, wishbones, pro sets, split-Ts, flankers and wide-outs, and so on.

To make sense out of the names for field hockey positions, a fan needs to remember that it is a game of constant movement in which the sides change from attack to defense and back again in a matter of moments and players "go both ways," as they say, changing roles and formations as quickly as the ball moves from stick to stick. In field hockey, there are no positions that are purely offensive or purely defensive. Even the goalkeeper's clearance kick is the start of her team's counter-attack. Each player has a job to do depending on where the ball is, who's got it, and which way it's moving. As hockey is played nowadays, Backs and Links (also called Midfielders or Halfs) regularly rotate into the very forefront of the attack, so that coaches expect their players to know how to perform in any position on the team, whatever their regular places may be. That's one of the attractions of the game.

Without going into all the different formations that field hockey can employ, such as the 5-3-2-1, the 4-2-3-1-1, the 3-3-3-1-1, and so on (for all that, see chapter nine), it can be said that, except for the Goalies, there are three kinds of players:

1. Mainly attacking players on the offensive front line, called Forwards, or Wings and Inners, or Outs and Inners, depending on the individual coach's philosophy. The generic term is Forwards. In a front of three, there will

be two Wings right and left, sometimes called Outside Forwards, and a Center-Forward in the middle. In a front of five, players called Inners between theWings and the Center-Forward are added to serve as bridgers between the Halfbacks and the Forwards and to support the attack. Speed of foot, quickness of perception and reaction, adroit offensive stick-work, sure fielding and passing on the move, and shooting and rebounding are the skills needed here. The main idea is to create scoring opportunities and to score on them as quickly and accurately as possible, without pausing or breaking stride. Wings not only center the ball to Inside For- wards for shots on goal but also cut for the striking circle themselves. The Center Forward needs to be able to "go both ways" in dribbling, passing, and receiving. She has, obviously, the best shot on goal, but is often employed as a decoy for the Inners. In the 5-3-2-1 formation the Center Forward is the principal play maker. Forwards and Wings must be able to run all day.

2. Attack-support and transitional or linking players, usually three in number (left, right, and center), variously called Halfbacks, or Links, or Midfielders, depending on the coach, are the second line, whose duties on both offense and defense require them to have greater speed coupled with endurance than anyone else on the field. They need to be good not only at passing but also at tackling opponents with the ball, intercepting opponents' passes and fielding one's own, guarding opponents (called marking), and cov- ering (backing up defenders). They enjoy wrecking the plans of their opposite numbers on the other side. Recently they've come to be used on attack more often than formerly, which has made good passing an even more important skill; but they've always been the mainstay of the transi- tional game. Nowadays Links may be asked to join Forwards on the attack in what is called overlapping. Traditionally Halfbacks do a lot of work on defense that no one sees, like getting back to cover or just taking up a position that will discourage an attacking maneuver by the other team. They also move quickly on turnovers to send the ball upfield to charging Wings and Forwards. People who want to see their names in headlines probably will not be happy as Links, but coaches are always grateful to these hard working and all too often unsung heroes.

3. Fullbacks, usually called Backs, are primarily defenders, but they play a crucial role in taking the ball away from an attacking opponent – typically the Inside Forwards – and starting a counter-attack. All the defensive skills of the Halfbacks are required here, in spades, not least the ability to anticipate and interfere with attackers' moves, tackle them, and intercept their passes. Really quick reflexes are needed to pounce on an attacker

so as to spoil a pass or shot on goal. Tackling, containing, jabbing, funneling an opponent to one sideline or the other, and retreating — thus the Back tries to keep the attacker from getting behind her or otherwise functioning as she wants to do. She never rushes a Forward in control lest she be through-passed, and she stays alert for passes to either side, thinking of all the ways there are of getting around a marker. Instant reaction is what's wanted here, not just to stop the attack but to get the ball and dispose of it to a teammate as fast and as accurately as she can. Through it all the Backs must be unflappable. Cool is the word.

Backs are the usual covering defenders who back up (cover) those markers guarding attacking opponents and try to help out if they get through. A Back marks Forwards attacking down her side of the field, and the Back on the other side comes over to cover behind and toward the center. When the attack moves to the other side, the Backs exchange positions.

A special Back, who plays immediately in front of the Goalkeeper and is her most important support when under attack, is sometimes called the Sweep or Sweeper. Speed is less important here than quickness, courage, decisiveness, and knowledge of the strengths and weaknesses of the attackers. Often it's the Sweeper who blocks the key shot, gets the key interception, clears the ball to one side of the field or another, backs up the Goalie, or follows a tackle with a pass upfield to a counter-attacking Back. It's often said that the Goalie is only as good as her Sweep. She's a one-woman set of Backs. Everything that defines them also describes the Sweep, whose relationship to the Goalie most be closely cooperative.

And then there's the Goalie, the loneliest player on the field most of the game except for those passages of violently stressful activity when she's under enemy attack.

The Goalie must be the bravest player on the team to advance to block the attackers' shots with her upper body or gloves, with her big leg pads, with a slide tackle (the splits to us), and then kick the ball out of danger to one side or the other with her stick (one-handed) or those big shoes she wears. She has to have a cat's quickness to follow the crazy ricochets of the ball, and she needs to know thoroughly how her own teammates, as well as her opponents, will react to every bounce and roll in the scuffle before the cage, in order to anticipate their moves and have a counter-measure ready. On penalty shots from the stroke line, it's Goalie against the opponents' best shooter of flicks from seven yards out, with just maybe the game on the line. On penalty corner it's five on five or more (theoretically) with the attackers standing on the edge of the striking circle ready to rush the ball when it's hit into play for a shot on goal. Definitely not a pleasant spot to be in!

That's why the Goalie has some advantages the other players don't. For one thing, the Goalie can stop an opponent's ball with any part of her body – even to the point of kicking it – without causing a penalty to be called. That is, as long as she stays inside the circle.

The Goalie's other advantage? Why, she's the best dressed player on the field – or the most dressed, at any rate.

However that may be, young hockey players ought to keep in mind some guidelines to good play, whatever position they occupy. For starters, remember that the position being played is not carved in granite for all posterity. A young player may discover that she's better at being a Link than a Forward, for example, or she may grow out of one position as her skills develop or the needs of her team take her in another direction. Players should try different positions in practice and see how they do. It's a good idea to get to know the basics, at least, of the other positions on the team, since that knowledge will improve an individual's play wherever she is. Then too, she might just be asked to play there!

By the same token, it is important to remember that all positions on a team are important, since winning depends on effective coordination of all eleven players on a side. To be sure, some players handle the ball more than others – Right Wings and Forwards for instance – but ball handling is far from being the index of importance to a team. Consider the Goalie, who handles the ball less than anyone (unless it is a very bad team indeed!) — yet her play is vital to the success of the team as a whole. One of the great truths of sports is that any position is only as important as the player in it can make it. There are no great positions, only great players.

Whatever your position, learn the fundamentals of good play there, the three or four or five things you must do to fulfill your role in the ensemble play that is team sport. If you have a part in a play, you can't afford to miss your cues, skip your entrances or exits, or forget your lines. Being a team player requires the same responsibilities: you don't have to be Sarah Bernhardt, you just have to be there, doing your thing in the scheme of things.

Since you're a beginner, you've got a lot to learn about the game and your place in it. That means you're going to make mistakes, you're not always going to achieve the goals you've set for yourself, somebody's going to beat you. Learning from your mistakes is how you become a better player. How do you do that? By reviewing your play after every practice session and game and critically evaluating your performance as objectively as you can. What parts of your game did you do well? Where do you need improvement? Put your conclusion down in your mind or on paper in a declarative statement. Ask your coach for an opinion, too, after you've made your assessment. You may be surprised by what you hear. Then work to improve. Above all, don't get down on yourself over your goofs. That'll just make things worse. And remember: tomorrow's another game.

Last, play the entire length and breadth of the field. Don't crowd on attack. That clogs up the field so that nothing can happen. If everybody follows the ball you end up in a slam-dance pit. Move the ball out to the Wings whenever you can: that creates open spaces on the field that make coverage difficult for the other team and helps your Wings to stay wide, where they belong. And use both sides of the field on attack, not just the right-hand side as you're tempted to do. That also makes it harder to defend and opens up lanes of attack.

Chapter Five
The Players: Moves

Field hockey is preeminently a game of swift and fluid movement. Good play combines speed afoot, quick execution, and precision and accuracy, thereby making it more a passing game than a dribbling and dodging game. Don't get puffed up if your team dribbles and dodges a lot: it may only mean that the field is too rough to accommodate a passing game or that your team still has a lot to learn about moving the ball about. To be sure, "good (or clever) stickwork" is a high compliment in this game, where it is an indispensable skill, but individual players are often prone to piddle around with the ball instead of doing something creative like passing it to a teammate who's broken free toward the goal. Such behavior is irritating as can be, and persistent offenders in this regard are taken deep into the woods by their coaches and lost. Sometimes they are found by ancient field hockey coaches, who often live in the woods after retiring. They cook them. That is not generally known.

All of which serves to remind us that field hockey is a game of spaces, of places where no defenders are which have been created by good offensive work. Both attack and defense are mainly trying to open up or close up such vacant areas or using them to the advantage of one side or the other. Watching field hockey thus requires more of participants and onlookers than do most other field sports. You need to be aware of what's going on all over the field of play and of how an attack and the defense against it are developing — simultaneously. Like chess, field hockey also requires players and spectators to look ahead a few moves.

A common theme running through the pages that follow concerns the various ways field hockey has come to terms with the right-to-left bias given to play by the asymmetrical design of the stick, with its flat striking face to the left. The problem of how to get the face of the stick to go from left to right effectively by finding ways to reverse it or to come around on the ball involves no less a matter than opening up the entire left half of the field to offensive and defensive operations. It gives players on that side of the field something to do and doubles the area that has to be defended. Being able to manipulate the stick so that it has two usable faces frees dribblers to carry or pass the ball either to the right or the left, thus complicating the defender's task. It also means that the coach will be heard pleading with her players to use both sides of the field on attack.

That reminds us of the most important rule about how to become a good field hockey player: learn your fundamentals and practice them at slow speed until you get them right. There's plenty of time to increase the speed of your play once you've learned how things should be done. That takes practice, lots of it. Learn it the way your coach wants it done. No bad habits of your own invention, please. Sometimes you can play better for a while doing something wrong than you can by doing it right; but over the long haul you'll be better off learning to make your moves by the numbers.

HANDLING YOUR STICK

You'll notice that players carry their sticks as though shaking hands with them, the left hand at the butt end of the grip and the right hand halfway down towards the other end, the flat side of the toe pointing forward or to the left. The juncture of the left forefinger and thumb forms an inverted "V" in line with the stickhead and its toe at the other end. The palm of the right hand is against the back of the stick. Surprisingly, the left hand actually controls the stick, turning it through an arc of more than 180-degrees as it opens or closes the face, while the right hand imparts power or steadiness to strokes and stops. That is why left-handed players are often so good with their sticks: being left-handed is a decided advantage in this game.

Reversing the stick counterclockwise (to the left) a half-circle (180 degrees), makes the flat side of the toe face to the right and the toe itself point to the rear. In dribbling and trapping (a.k.a receiving or intercepting) situations, coaches teach their players to hold the stick in the left hand with the "V" rotated a half-turn to the right in such a way as to facilitate reversal. It's awkward at first, but the advantage of rapid stick reversal makes it worthwhile, and eventually you'll get used to it. The rest of the time you can carry your stick in the usual position.

Reversing the stick is also necessary if you want to do the Indian dribble, which involves moving the ball left and right, back and forth between the flat stick side on the right and the reversed stick side on the left as you advance up and down the field. It's hard to do, particularly on a rough surface, but once you've mastered the Indian dribble you can beat your opponent with it by the freedom it gives you to pass, shoot, drive or move to the right or left almost instantaneously.

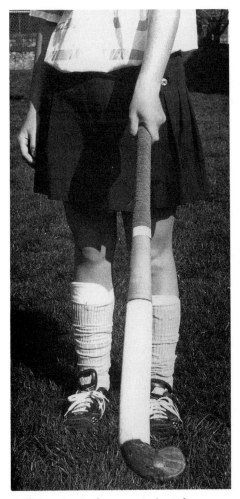 

Left-hand grip for reversed stick   **Left-hand grip (stick-side)**

Standard grip (two hands)

One other point: don't tense up on your stick. Your grip should be light enough to feel your stickhead as you push, hit, or field the ball. And try to keep your arms and shoulders just as light and loose, too.

In any case, a good player moves with her head up and knees bent for maximum balance and freedom of movement and direction, the toe of the stick touching the ground, and the stick held at an angle appropriate to the condition of the field. The rule is, the rougher the surface, the more nearly perpendicular the stick — the better to field high or eccentric bounces. Hence, if you're a spectator don't yell "Sticks down!" at your team until you've first sized up the playing field.

STROKES

Hitting

Perhaps the simplest shot in field hockey is the hit or drive (the all-out wallop). Because a hitter can use a back-swing and follow-through, this stroke is powerful and can carry the ball a great distance at great speed, although a well-timed transfer of body weight from back to front and wrist snap should make a big wind-up and after-swing unnecessary. Hence the drive's use in clearing the ball a long way upfield to relieve a defense under pressure, to gain a deep stretch of territory quickly for Forwards and Links to exploit, especially on a long corner shot or a sixteen-yard hit, to pass to an attacking teammate, to execute a set play, or to take a shot on goal.

For a drive, you slip your right hand up the stick to join your left at the top, holding the stick very much as though it were a golf driver. Doing this means that you straighten your back a bit from the usual way you carry yourself at the ready, since more of the stick is exposed, but your head should still be, as always, directly over the ball and your eyes focused on it. Your body should be "side-on" to the ball: that is, your left shoulder should be pointed in the direction of the intended stroke and your body parallel to it, a bit to the side, and slightly behind the ball, your feet comfortably apart — say about the width of your shoulders. You want the ball to be off your left heel. The stroke itself involves employing the swing of your stick to transfer the weight of your body from your right (rear) foot to your left (front) foot at the same time that the head of your stick meets the ball. (A tip: if the toe of your stick is pointed up at the peak of your back-swing and at the end of your follow-through, chances are you'll hit the ball squarely.)

Backswing

Impact

Follow-through

In a perfect world, the ball, like the proverbial speeding bullet, should skim just above the ground for a great distance, while your stick completes its graceful follow-through in front of you. The spectators utter an awestruck "oooooo" of admiration. Teammates smile. Unfortunately, in the real world, things can go wrong. If you neglect to aim well, your best shot can be stopped short by an alert opponent's block, and an attack begins. You can get your stick ahead of the ball and top it, causing the ball to dissipate its momentum in a weak hit. If you hit behind the ball or undercut it, you can cause it to loft – anywhere above the knees is too high – and pose a threat of hitting a player in the head or some other sensitive place where a serious injury might result. You'll be penalized, besides. By the same token, if you're careless about going too high on your back-swing or follow-through – above the shoulders, to be specific – you run the risk of hurting someone with your stick, perhaps seriously. In either case, an official will call you for undercutting or dangerous play and your team will get a penalty. Persistent carelessness with stick or ball can get you carded — or worse. A certain latitude is allowed on "sticks" if you're hitting in a space clear of other players and if the ball goes into a relatively vacant area.

The Running Hit

The hits we've been discussing so far are largely made by players who are stationary, or nearly so, on clearances; but given the great speed of the modern game of field hockey, more and more drives are made while running, as passes to teammates or shots on goal. Running hits are made as stationary hits are — off the left foot with the swing of the stick coinciding smoothly with the thrust of the stride, eyes on the ball and the rest of it. But because the shooter is in traffic, the arc of the stick must be under much greater control to help maintain the balance needed for accuracy and for safety's sake. The back-swing must not be wild, high, or ragged but controlled and limited, and the follow-through measured. It's not only a matter of trying to avoid a referee's call of "Sticks!" You want to make that pass precise and at playable speed. The most common mistake novice hockey players make is in passing the ball much too hard for another novice, who is also playing on a bumpy field, to receive without fumbling. In field hockey the key words are sharp, crisp, quick, accurate, and fast.

Hitting Off-Balance

As the pace of the game picks up, the need to drive off the wrong foot and off-balance, as opportunities present themselves, becomes more urgent. We wish we had a simple formula for such hits, but there aren't any. Suffice it to say, try to strike from the side and off the heel of your forward foot, to keep your head over the ball and your eyes on it, and choke down on your stick for greater control and speed of execution. Later, as your skill grows, you'll learn how to turn your wrists at impact to alter the direction, height, or speed of your drives, even when they're off the wrong foot. Stick control, they call it. Like hitting off balance, it's an advanced skill.

Pushing

Often when you have the ball, you'll just push it with your stick, instead of hitting it. That's a legitimate stroke, often used to vary the pace of advancing the ball and thus to fake out a marker. Because the push needs no backstroke, indeed, must not have one, and the stick is carried in the "ready" position, with hands apart, it can be employed as a weapon of surprise or deception, to make a soft pass to a teammate or, as on a penalty corner or a side-in, to move the ball in an unexpected direction. It is the stroke of the set play, where quick disposal and disguised intent are most wanted. When done properly, the stick face stays against the ball for maximum control, even though novice players on rough fields will move the ball ahead with a series of light taps— always at risk of interception, of course, if the ball gets too far ahead of the stick.

Using the usual lefthand grip, the push is made from a half-crouch, with knees flexed, body side-on to the ball, which at the moment of impact should be off the left heel, the head over the ball and eyes on it, and stick face against the ball. Since there's no backlift of the stick, this stroke gains its strength from the explosive forward push of the right hand while the left moves in the opposite direction, back toward the body. Done right, the left foot should point in the direction you want the ball to go, and the force of the stroke should come from the rapid transfer of weight from the right foot in the rear to the left foot in front, together with the low, forward follow-through. Note that you can push off the "wrong" – that is, the right – foot, too, especially if you're on the left side of the field and passing to your right. In that case, move your feet to get around on the ball and make sure that your upper body turns right as well. Make sure your eyes stay on the ball all the way through the push. Follow-through is important.

Common mistakes include bending at the waist, weakness in the right hand, wrist, or arm, left arm resistance, faulty body-ball relation, poor coordination between thrust of the right arm and the forward shift of body weight, poor follow-through, and lifting the head before hitting the ball. Sounds a lot like golf, doesn't it?

FLICKS AND SCOOPS

You can loft a field hockey ball, of course, if you're playing in high school (but not in college), and when you do so it's called a flick or a scoop. Like the push, flicks and scoops are made without a back-swing, by tucking the bottom edge of the flat stick face, which is inclined upwards, under the back side of the ball and thrusting it sharply upward and forward. Like the drive, flicks and scoops are usually made standing. Flicks are shots lofted on goal from the penalty stroke line. Well placed in an upper corner of the cage, they're hard for goalkeepers to reach. A flick has much more power behind it and a flatter trajectory than a scoop, which is usually higher and slower and comes off a stroke that resembles the thrust one makes when shoveling snow.

Scoops occur in field action, most often when putting the ball in play on a free-hit after a turnover. They're allowed because they're a great way of getting the ball safely over and past a line of defenders to some teammates on the other side, but not when sending a free hit into the striking circle. That's illegal.

Scoop stick position

Scoop follow-through

You make a flick by holding your left hand close to your body and moving your right hand well down the stick to gain leverage and elevation for the stroke. At the beginner's level, you really spread and crouch side-on to the ball, which at the point of contact should be off the left heel. Your right foot is well back, to serve as a steadying or anchoring brace, but not so far back that you can't generate much forward thrust when the stroke moves your weight to the front. Good balance is what's wanted here.

Although not as powerful as a drive, a flick or scoop can have enough force behind it to hurt, so hitting one directly into an opponent can prompt a foul call. Properly hit, a scoop should clear players' heads by a good three to six feet: any higher can give opponents an opportunity to get under and intercept it. By the way, you'll notice that defenders can field a scoop in mid-air with a hand, even catch it, providing that they don't advance the ball in doing so. It must drop directly from hand to ground. That's called a handstop, and it's made with the fingers spread, the hand cupped, and the arm relaxed. The handstop is the only situation in this game in which a part of the body can be used defensively without fouling — goalkeepers excepted of course. NCAA field hockey, however, is a no-hands-at-all game.

Flick: stick position   **Flick: follow through**

One step flick series (advanced)

FIELDING

Receiving the ball, from whatever source, is called fielding or trapping or stopping, which includes taking a pass from a teammate or making an interception of an opponent's pass. Fielding involves more than simply stopping the ball: it includes protecting the ball and positioning it for immediate aggressive play. To facilitate fielding, you'll notice, defending players carry their sticks as nearly parallel to the ground as comfort and the playing surface allow. The right hand should be halfway or more down the stick, so that the heel of the palm is firmly lodged against the back of the stick. The lefthand grip is the same as that for a reversed stick. The rougher the field the more nearly perpendicular the stick needs to be carried – the better to stop high bounces. Keeping the right hand well down on the stick maximizes the options available to the fielder.

In fielding you want to look the ball into your stick; scanning the wider field of play can go on before and after. Let the ball come to the stick so that the right hand feels its arrival at the stick's face and cushions the impact. By this time the stickhead should be resting on the ground, and "hooded" – its face inclined in the direction of the ball. It is angled across the front of the body, with the left hand in front of the left hip and the right hand knee high. Try to take the ball in front of or off the right foot, feet either facing in the direction the ball comes or with the left foot pointed in that direction while the right is at right angles to its path.

Fielding requires accurate passing as well as sure stickwork, just as in football a fast, sticky-fingered flanker needs a quarterback who can put the ball on his numbers. A properly passed ball should reach a fielder at a speed that can be handled, on her flat stick side, and comfortably in front of the right foot. For her part, the fielder shouldn't be standing there flat-footed, though she needn't be running all-out either; but she must be ready to do something creative with the ball when it arrives — preferably to pass it. On the left-hand side of the field, to avoid the contortions required to receive a pass on the flat side of the stick, passes can be taken on the reversed stick side, with the fielder side-on to the ball, if she's moving, well over the ball, and with her body in balance. At the level of play we're concerned with in these pages, we want to concentrate on doing what we do well. In the passing game, that means trying to make our passes go from one flat stick to another flat stick if at all possible.

Looking up before the ball arrives is a common mistake in receiving, as is reaching out for balls better taken by moving the feet to get position and having the wrong grip.

Having a "cinder-block stick," like "hard hands" in football, can cause the ball to rebound out of control (six inch max), and bad stickwork in general – not being ready, stick too high, bad stickhead angle, trying to be cute, and the like – can result in a fumble. There's nothing fancy about receiving: just keep your eye on the ball, line it up, and let it come to a stationary stick. Keep it simple!

Reverse stick pass and reception

Pass left to right, reception from left on right

Reverse-stick reception

DRIBBLING

When we speak of dribbling in field hockey, it has nothing to do with what your baby brother does when he drinks out of his milk-cup. Yuck! Dribbling here means moving a ball under the control of your stick while running at various speeds and in various directions on the field of play — hopefully as part of a coordinated scheme to score a goal or to accomplish something else worth-while. That something can be as simple as keeping possession of the ball or clearing it upfield after a turnover. Since any team sport is the sum total of many individual engagements, dribbling can be a tactic by which to out-maneuver an opponent in order to make something else happen — to assist a successful pass, to cause an opponent to commit a foul, to get by her for a shot on goal, whatever. Dribbling and passing are the most-done actions on a hockey field.

Straight dribbling, the most common kind, differs from hitting and pushing in that it requires a more wide-open stance. You're not side-on so much in dribbling. Instead, the ball is kept more nearly in front of you, a bit to the right of your right foot. The farther out in front of the feet the ball is, the faster you can run and, hence, dribble; but you're more vulnerable to tackles. The inverted "V" formed by the thumb and forefinger of your left hand should be rotated slightly to the right of your usual grip in order to allow a smooth transition to a reversed stick when needed. Your hands should be well apart on the stick, the right loosely and comfortably down the stick about halfway or a little more. Too far down means better control but reduced vision; too far up means better vision but less control. You must find your own "comfort zone." Your left forearm forms a straight extension of the stick, which is angled forward so that your right hand is farther from your body than the left. Your back should be fairly straight, your head up, knees flexed and ready to move right or left, weight balanced, and eyes on the ball. The ball is played in front of your body, notice, so that you can pass left deceptively and, if you can reverse stick effectively, pass right as well.

At the risk of repeating ourselves, let us emphasize that learning to reverse your stick instantly and use it as deftly as a flat stick is an essential skill in hockey and as such requires long practice, tempered by competition, to perfect. Not everyone who reads these pages will become an accomplished stick reverser, but you all should be able to dribble successfully with a flat stick, not tapping the ball along as you will do at first but cradling it in the toe of your stick and pretty well being able to do what you want to with it, smoothly and almost effortlessly. Even if you are a master of the reversed stick, you will want to vary your play from the left by using footwork to position the face of your flat stick in the direction you want the ball to go. It's always possible to open the face of your stick for plays to the right.

Dribbling: grip rotated to the right

Common errors in dribbling include an incorrect grip, a too-upright stick, often with a break at the wrist, a ball played too close to the feet, failing to stay down on turns, and ball-watching — that is, not scanning enough to see the field of play. (Learning to use your peripheral vision can prove to be very helpful in seeing both ball and field.) Getting too close to a defender leaves a dribbler with little room in which to dodge or maneuver.

For example, the pullback dribble is one of the oldest dodges in the game. About four or five feet from a defender the dribbler suddenly makes a sharp – not rounded – 90-degree turn left or right. If the defender doesn't follow the turn, the dribbler turns upfield and accelerates. If the defender follows the dribbler, the dribbler drags or pulls the ball back in the opposite (diagonal) direction and does a drop step away from the defender before turning sharply upfield and accelerating or passing. A triangle is done like the pullback except that the pullback part is preceded by a drag left or right across the front of the body. These maneuvers force the defender to commit herself, and force the dribbler to "read" the defender's position and distance so as to make the right cut. They must be done quickly, with one touch of the stick, not two. As in all good dribbling, the stick stays with the ball and control is easy and relaxed: there's no swinging. A dribbler needs poise and patience and the ability to see how she can use empty spaces to her advantage and how to recognize an opponent's commitment to an exploitable position or movement. Nimble footwork is essential.

Passing off a dribble is a key play in this game. A good dribble puts you where you can make a clever pass. Passing off a dribble, while you're moving, requires that you hit off the wrong (the right-hand) foot, whereas passing to the right is easiest done by making a quarter turn to the right and passing off the flat stick as you plant your left foot.

Then there's the Indian Dribble spoken of earlier, which consists of moving the ball back and forth from the flat stick side to the reversed stick side while zigzagging rapidly up the field and scanning for opportunities to beat an opponent or pass to an open teammate. Yes, that's right: you do all that at the same time. To do the Indian Dribble requires that from the flat stick side you push off your right foot, with the ball ahead and inside your right foot so that it can be moved toward your left side, where it is received by the reversed stick. To return it, you push off your left foot to go ahead, playing the ball from inside and ahead of the left foot. This maneuver requires years of practice to do well, but when mastered it gives the dribbler the advantage over a defender of being able to pass or move without hesitation in any direction to the side or front.

Indian dribble: push from stick side   **Indian dribble: push off reversed stick side**

If you're very lucky, or a very deceptive dribbler, you may lure the opponent who is marking you into charging at the ball or otherwise over-committing herself. When that happens you can pass the ball by her and pick it up again, or you can sidestep and let her go on by while you head off up the field. Its up to you!

PASSING

The art of passing is such an intimate part of this game that it has been an important topic in most of the subjects we've discussed so far, whatever their heading may have been. Hitting, pushing, and flicking, for example, are all passes. A basic rule of field hockey is that the best way to beat a defender is to pass the ball by her or around her. The greatest weakness of field hockey in the United States is our lack of a passing game. The great national teams overseas are accomplished passers.

Why pass? To keep the initiative by forcing defenders to stay in motion and to re-adjust constantly, so they can only react to attackers' gambits. To move the ball more quickly than dribbling. To maintain possession of the ball. To gain a territorial advantage. To penetrate opponents' defenses and eliminate defenders by outmaneuvering them. And, what is much the same thing, to change the point of attack so as to make defensive schemes pointless or misplaced. In other words, to gain a trick by finessing.

Every pass is different. Even so, certain everyday varieties of passes have been given names which are part of the lingo of the game, and young players need to know what they are and how to do them. Notice how passing and deception go hand in hand. That's why you want to use the reversed stick grip.

The **SQUARE (OR FLAT) PASS** is made to a teammate coming up on one side or the other when you've got the ball and face an opponent's marker in front and a cover farther back. Think of it as you would a lateral in football – a way to keep the ball while changing the direction of play and finessing defenders.

The **THROUGH PASS** is made straight ahead through a gap in the defense to a teammate who has gotten into an empty space behind the opponents in front of you. Your pass should lead your teammate so that she can receive it as she cuts upfield.

The **DIAGONAL PASS** is made to a teammate who is cutting through an uncovered space between two defenders.

The **BACK PASS** is a 45-degree pass made to the rear on either side for the same purpose as the flat pass.

In the **GIVE-AND-GO**, just as in basketball, a marked attacker passes off to a teammate on one side, then cuts around the marker and takes a pass right back from her teammate.

The **OVERLAP** pass is when a marked attacker dribbles to the left, say, to open up the space just vacated, then square passes to a teammate charging upfield through the opening.

The **BACK DOOR** is also similar to a basketball play. A marked attacker dribbles to the right, say, to open up a space on the left. Then a teammate cuts behind the ball-handler, breaks upfield, and receives a square pass.

Let us repeat an admonition you're probably getting sick of hearing: young players of field hockey should pass to the flat stick side of their teammates, and receivers should try to position themselves so as to receive the ball on their flat stick side. Why? It's easier for inexperienced players to handle, whether passing or fielding, while you're practicing the really tough moves.

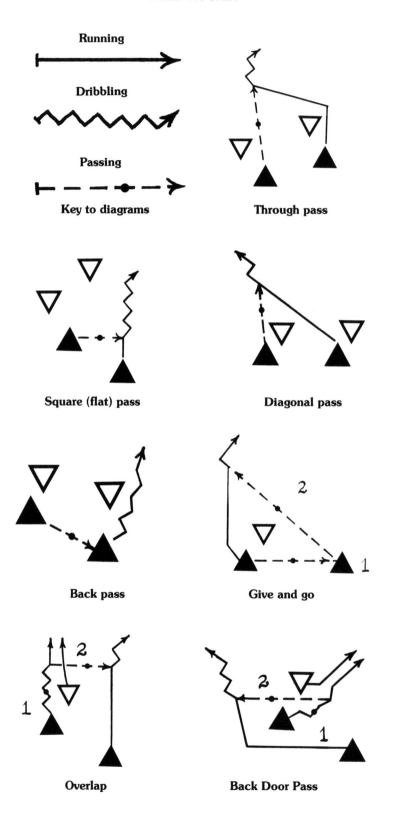

Running

Dribbling

Passing

Key to diagrams

Through pass

Square (flat) pass

Diagonal pass

Back pass

Give and go

Overlap

Back Door Pass

What is a good pass? A ball that reaches its receiver so that possession is kept, a ball that arrives at the very moment that the receiver does, and a ball that can be taken without any break in the motion of the receiver toward the opponents' goal. To be more specific, good passing means passing earlier than most American players want to do, when they're three or four yards away from an opponent. Making the simple pass to the obvious receiver is usually best. Passing firmly, briskly, crisply, and neither too hard to field nor too soft to get there, is the way to do it. Being able to get free from an opponent to make a pass, and knowing how to cut so as to receive a pass free of an opponent — these are key skills. Timing, of course, is crucial, particularly speed of execution. Be decisive.

DODGES

As to dodges, we've discussed pulls, pull-backs, and the various kinds of passes and dribbles designed to baffle defenders. Feints or fakes as such, in the narrowest senses of those terms, are any maneuver of your head, body, feet, stick, or ball that deceives a defender into thinking that something will be done with the ball which does not occur. This is done by pretending to offer the defender an opportunity which, when she tries to seize it, you withdraw, taking the ball elsewhere. What you do with the ball once you've suckered your marker in — that's the dodge. It's a way of getting around an opponent. We're familiar with broken-field runners in football who put out a foot as though to plant it, only to plant the other and be off in an unexpected direction. So in field hockey. In addition to wrong-footing, hip-slipping, and moving the head or shoulders so as to falsely indicate a change in direction or speed, and manipulating the face of the stick head to deceive, acceleration is as much a part of the dodge as mis-direction. Speeding up can frustrate your opponent's tackle-back, a move she's sure to make after she turns the ball over. Just to put things into perspective, let us repeat the old adage that the best dodge is a good pass: crisp passing teams don't need dodges. But dodges are useful for young teams on bad fields; and bad fields are what we mostly play on in school hockey, more's the pity.

The aptly named "Y-dodge" is a movement that inscribes an invisible letter "Y" on the field when you do it. Dribbling toward a defender with the ball on your stick side, you fake a turn to your left, hit your ball in the opposite direction back to the marker's non-stick side, and then go around to pick it up and proceed upfield, having left your opponent behind with your fake.

Y-dodge: approach

Y-dodge: pass to left

Y-dodge: retrieve ball and cut upfield

There are also a couple of pulls, one to the right and one to the left. In the first, start by moving your stick or the ball 90 degrees to the left, then come back to the right with it, pick the ball up, and dribble on upfield with it past your defender's non-stick side. Notice what we're saying here: it's entirely possible to leave the ball in the grass, pass your empty stick over it as if you were dribbling to the left, while your marker follows the motion of your stick enough to be drawn out of position. That leaves the ball free for your return to move it around the other side. This is a stick-fake, pure and simple. The same deception can be worked in the opposite direction, against your marker's stick side.

Dodge: pull to left

Dodge: pull to right

DEFENSE

Marking

All this talk about hitting, lofting, dodging and the like serves to remind us that there's another side to field hockey than attacking. It's called defense. Defenders likewise have their moves, in addition to marking – that is, guarding – attackers in man-to-man or zone coverage, or in a combination of the two not unlike some defensive formations in basketball. One of the most easily spotted is a kind of marking called "ballside and goalside," meaning that the defender in a one-on-one situation assumes a position vis-a-vis the attacker that is simultaneously between the ball and the opponent and between the opponent and the goal. That is, being ballside means taking up a position where you can get to the ball first; being goalside means occupying a place that, if you miss the ball, allows you still to remain between the ball and the goal. That's the catbird seat, and good Sweeps and Defenders are adept at putting themselves in it. It embodies the basic rule of all good field hockey defense: stand between your immediate opponent and your goal in a spot that gives you the greatest freedom to tackle or intercept. This involves being aware of the space behind you that the attacker wants to enter by going by or around you so that she can take a pass there.

Ballside and goalside

When marking, it's a good idea to watch the ball instead of the attacker, who may try to fake you in one of the ways we've seen, reversing directions and changing speed. Try to be alert and well forward on the balls of your feet, ready to move quickly in any direction. Keep your weight balanced. If possible, be where you can tackle on your stick side. Don't forget: you can disrupt you opponent's dribble or passes simply by faking lunges, blocks, and jabs. Crowd her into a sideline or another defender. You can play your opponent closer if you're a left-side defender going against a right-side attacker than you can if you're a right-side defender marking a left-side attacker. Be patient. Rushing an attacker may give her the opening to slip around you as you're going by and be off to the races.

Defense

Covering

What about covering, you ask? Good question. To cover is to support a teammate who has marked an opponent with the ball by backing her up on one side or the other, literally covering the space to the side and rear by forestalling all those overlaps, give-and-goes, and dodges we've been discussing. If your marker is beaten by an attacker, your job as cover may be to become the marker until a teammate can recover or fill in on the assignment you just had to vacate. Above all, you don't want an unmarked opponent to get loose with the ball near the goal, or, which is the same thing, for the attackers to achieve a numerical superiority over the defenders — three on two or four on three, say. In the interlocking diagonal formations favored by many field hockey coaches these days, a player who is covering a teammate on one side is probably marking an attacker on the other side. Trying to keep both tasks in proper balance can pose a nice dilemma for the player. You and your coach and teammates may have to agree about how far you can go in filling each assignment, knowing that detailed adjustments must be made on an ad hoc basis. The main idea remains: discourage attackers trying to get through or around you on one flank, and help your teammate to contain her attacker.

In a larger sense, marking is a form of man-to-man defense, as we said before; covering is zonal. It's possible to play "man," just as it's theoretically possible to play all zone. Most cases combine man and zone in a configuration like that we just examined.

Tackling

When you get right down to it, defense is tackling an opponent who has the ball, in hopes of getting it away from her, or putting so much pressure on her that she hits a bad pass, or simply harassing her into ineffectuality or into committing a foul when she tries to tackle-back. Tackling is done with your stick, aimed at the ball in those moments when it is away from contact with your opponent's stick. If your stick strikes the ball-carrier's stick you'll be called for interference.

Nowadays tackling per se is not emphasized as it once was, since many coaches think that, with less risk of fouling, much can be accomplished instead by going for interceptions, containing attackers through delaying tactics till the defense is in place, and funneling dribblers into covering backs, a sideline, or a relatively useless space. Nevertheless, the straight-on tackle – really a block – is often employed against an oncoming dribbler when the ball is off her stick. The tackler should be in a relatively open stance like her opponent, lined up on the right foot and facing the attacker, with the stick down as if dribbling but at the angle dictated by field conditions. You literally put your stick in the way of the ball and capture it on the face of your club, while the dribbler goes on by. If you've ever seen a basketball player set up at the last second to take a charge you'll understand what precise timing the tackler needs to bring off this move without getting called for hacking. Young players do a lot of hacking.

A lunge is another piece of work altogether, since it involves having the speed to get far enough ahead of an opposing dribbler on her right side – and close enough – to reach the ball with your stick. The idea is to reach into the area in front of the attacker's stick where the ball is being played and knock or pull it out without interfering with the other's stick, lest you get called for interference or obstruction. The actual act of reaching the ball can be done one-handedly, left-handedly, although you should keep both hands on the stick as much as possible. Keep your stick as low and at the best angle field conditions allow, to cover changes in the ball's direction should your opponent make them, as she certainly will try to do. Everything depends on the quickness of your thrust. Strike when the ball is away from the dribbler's stick, since the foul involves putting yourself or your stick between your opponent and the ball.

Tackling: block (straight-on) good field conditions

Tackling: reversed stick block (straight-on)

Tackling: block stick position for rough field conditions

A "wrongside tackle" or "circular tackle" on the reversed-stick side of an opposing ball-carrier is another option if you are faster than she. Here again you need to get close to and at least even with the dribbler, then maneuver your shoulders and feet around so as to be able to reach your stick into the path of the ball when it's being played away from the stick and pick it off without fouling. Aside from hitting her stick, the danger here is in hooking your opponent's stick with the toe of your stick. Another important use of this procedure is, by keeping up pressure on her non-stick side, to funnel an advancing opponent into one of your team's defenders who's already there, waiting to mark. You then go on by and become the covering back. An elegantly economic move, like a proof in math.

Then there's the "reverse stick tackle," which also requires that you be fast enough to get your shoulders ahead of the dribbler on her left side and reach in with your stick reversed and pull the ball out while it is being played off the stick — all without hacking the attacker's stick. Great nicety of timing is called for here.

Circular tackle

Reverse stick tackle

Reverse stick pullout

Funneling (stick-side)

A tackle is not an easy movement to make successfully. Bad tackling includes being caught flat-footed and faked out of your socks instead of being on your toes and balanced. Approaching an opponent too openly face-on instead of a bit side-on leaves you vulnerable to a pass through or around you, as does charging. Charging, as we have seen, also gives your opponent an invitation to sidestep while you barrel on by, so that she can then continue up the field. You're left standing there. To avoid that embarrassment, stay balanced and on your toes and take short steps: that gives you a chance to retreat and reposition should an opponent's fakes and dodges cause you to miss a tackle first time round. You can slow an attack down – it's called containing – simply by making a stubborn retreat and harassing your opponent by jabbing your stick and faking tackles. You always want to tackle with the flat side of your stick if possible, not end-on with the toe, for fear of hooking.

In general, it's a good practice to let your attacking opponent make the first move, not you: that commits her to some line of action, which in turn gives you time to size it up and react. To repeat an earlier point: try to use your tackling to channel or funnel your opponent in the direction you want her to go, even if you can't get at the ball. You overplay on the side you want your attacker to avoid, encourage her to take the easy way out — the way you want her to go. That's channeling or funneling. It helps slow down an attack and give your teammates more time to get back on defense. Finally, one more time: when tackling keep the head of your stick low.

TRANSITIONS

This is as good a time as any to stress the importance of immediate response to any change of possession of the ball. Starting an attack going up field the instant your team gets a turnover, getting back on defense and setting up just as soon as you lose the ball to the other side — these are the marks of a really good field hockey team. Or any other kind of team, for that matter.

A key element in the transition game consists in not giving up after you've been beaten by an opposing player. If you lose the ball on a turnover, tackle-back at the first opportunity, if possible before your opponent has achieved perfect control of the ball. That's probably your best chance at the ball. In any event, challenge the other side and contest their progress, the moment they come into possession of the ball, all the way back down the field.

Stay on your opposite number, marking, tackling, harassing, every step. In marking, covering, dribbling, and passing, sheer persistence is an indispensable quality for a player to have. Just staying on top of the ball, worrying your opponent, makes up for a multitude of technical weaknesses. Be a terrier.

TALKING

As fast as modern hockey is played, communicating between teammates is essential. You should be in touch with each other constantly on offense and defense, warning of opponents' threats and calling attention to opportunities, asking for the ball when you have an open field, or telling a teammate to take it when her chances are better, and so on. If you've been well coached, most of this give-and-take need not be verbal: a gesture or a look may be all you need. Indeed, if you're where you're supposed to be, your teammate with the ball will already be looking for you there. You should hardly ever have to call for the ball out loud, although letting a teammate know you're covering behind her is valuable. "I have your back!" said loudly enough to be heard is all that's needed. In front of your own net your goal-tender will tell you how to help her on defense. Voiced encouragement to a teammate, like "Great play, Jenny!" or "Better luck next time, Beth!," is important, of course, but not if it interferes with play. A gesture or pat on the back can say as much. Constant chatter afield is in most cases counterproductive, since it merely adds to the confusion. Don't call for the ball unless you're actually open, lest you end up like the little boy who cried "Wolf!" too often. Talk only when you have something really important to say. Don't "trash talk" your opposite number. If she does, ignore her. A bad mouth can get you carded.

SCANNING

During all the activities outlined above you are supposed to be keeping your eyes on the ball at the same time that you are scanning the field for threatening opponents and for play-making opportunities among your teammates. We know of a lizard that can simultaneously move one eye forward and the other eye backward, and spiders, who are notorious hotdogs, have eight eyes. But we don't know many people who can keep their eyes on the ball and on the field at the same time. Even so, all authorities unite in saying you must keep moving your eyes from ball to field and back again — AND NOT LOSE CONTROL OF THE BALL! It can get pretty hairy to dribble on a rough field, we know. We haven't a clue about showing you a neat way to do this successfully. You just learn to do it by doing it. Good luck!

SET PLAYS

In field hockey, as in most sports, there are set plays, many of which are crucial to scoring. In football we think of the field goal, kick-off, punt, and the like. Field hockey has its own set plays and they have assumed an ever larger place in scoring here of late.

When a ball is hit or bounces out of bounds (called a side-out), the team that last touched the ball loses possession of it, and the other team gets to put it into play at the spot it went out. That's called a side-in, hit-in, or push-in, and it's like an in-bounds play in basketball. That is, the ball is placed down on the sideline at the place it went out and hit out to a teammate afield to restart play. Your major task on a side-in play is to make sure the ball is not intercepted by the other team. Your coach is likely to have some plays drawn for side-ins under various conditions, both offensive and defensive.

The usual penalty for a foul committed outside the striking circle is a free hit: the ball is spotted at the site of the infraction and a member of the victimized team hits, pushes, or lofts it – forward, backward, sideways, over the rainbow – to restart play. The free hit is one of those occasions when the hitter will have that golden opportunity in field hockey to haul off and really swat the ball. Be our guest. But keeping possession of the ball may be your primary consideration. In that case, look to a good pass. Don't waste time on free hits; don't slow the pace of the game. Field hockey, like soccer, is a game that should flow.

You'll see a lot of side-ins and free hits in this game, for reasons that will soon become obvious. Notice that in such situations opposing players in the field must stay five yards away from the ball until it's put into play.

A 16-yard hit is awarded the defending team when the ball crosses the end line during an attack on goal after being played off an attacker's stick or after accidentally bouncing off a defender's stick on a shot from outside the 25-yard line. A defender gets to move the ball upfield from a place adjoining where the ball went out anywhere up to 16 yards out from the end line. You don't have to take the full 16 yards if you don't want to, but most do. If you can't find a teammate open for a pass you may want to indulge your passion for mighty wallops, but look for her first anyway. There are few things more pointless than a drive into empty space.

One of the most common set plays in hockey comes as a penalty against the defenders inside the striking circle. It's called a penalty corner, or just "corner" for short. The ball is placed on the defenders' end line not less than ten yards from the closest corner post of the goal cage. There are hashmarks to indicate the spots. Usually a Forward of the attackers, called the Hitter, is designated to pass the ball in to one of (usually) four (or more) other attacking players stationed around and just outside the edge of the striking circle, whose aim is to field the pass and drive it into the goal for a score. (They don't HAVE to be Forwards, by the way.) This player is called the Striker. Sometimes the pass-in is first handled by the Stickstopper, who does what her title implies and immediately gives up the ball to the Striker. Four defenders plus the Goalie, however, are positioned behind the end line in and around the cage. They rush out upon the attackers when the ball is put into play and try to frustrate their intentions by marking, tackling, covering, blocking or general intimidation. One or two of them can be stationed inside the goal cage until the pass-in, after which they step out and stand ready in front of the corner posts of the cage, backing up the Goalie, who has boldly advanced well into the circle to confront the Striker. That's why these two are called Post Players. While all this is going on, the rest of the defenders have retreated to positions behind the center line at midfield, while the attackers back up their teammates on the circle.

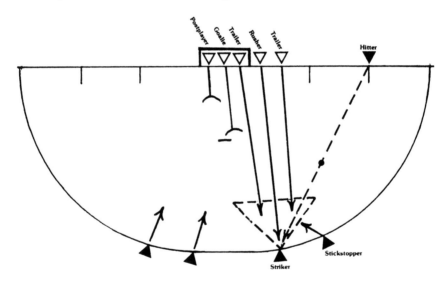

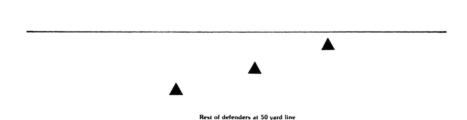

Rest of defenders at 50 yard line

Set play: penalty corner

The fastest player of the defenders' team is the designated Rusher, whose job it is to mark the Striker and force her into making bad layoffs (passes to teammates) or bad shots on goal. She stands to the left of the Goalie and to the left of the anticipated Striker. She runs out with the stick in her right hand and in line with the shot, so as not to block the Goalie's view of the ball. The remaining defenders, the Trailers, dash out ten yards and try to spread confusion in the ranks of the enemy: intercept layoffs, tackle a shooter, clear a ball from the circle, or pick up a rebound off the Goalie's pads. The Trailer to the side of the hit must be alert for a pass back to the Hitter, a venerable but still effective scoring ploy. So is the pass across the front of the cage to a shooter left unmarked by all the activity on the other side.

Corners, along with penalty strokes, provide some of the most exciting moments of the game. With topnotch players, on a truly level playing surface, a penalty corner score is about as certain as a field goal in football. On the kind of field most school teams have to put up with, scores on corners are unpredictable.

Another standard set play commonly used by the attackers is called centering the ball, in which the outside Forwards (or Wings), who have brought the ball downfield in their alleys along the side lines, as they're supposed to do, now drive it straight across the field parallel to the end line and into the striking circle, where one of the other Forwards, or the opposite Wing, can field it and fire it into the cage for a goal.

Finally, there are Goalkeepers. However, we'll save them for a chapter of their own.

Chapter Six
The Players: Keeping Goal

Once upon a time, the Goalkeeper was the worst athlete on the team, and the position of Goalie was treated with contempt. No more. In today's field hockey, the Goalie is as important as in the NHL. Her play is crucial on corners and penalty strokes. Because she alone among her teammates commands a view of the entire field, the Goalie can direct the defense by her instructions. She should be a student of the game, because her special position on the team endows her statements at team meetings and on the field with special weight and authority. It also helps if she has understanding parents.

Because of the peculiar difficulties and responsibilities of her position, the Goalie has to have a mixture of qualities. She must be brave, bold and yet cautious, reflexively quick, smart, alert and watchful throughout the match, agile, strong, intimidating, knowledgeable about the game and the players — and blessed with the self-confidence of one who is truly her own person. She has to get to know her position so well that, under attack, she plays with a fierce, intuitive concentration faster by far than conscious thought. She has one purpose: to prevent the ball from entering the cage, whatever it takes.

The Goalie needs to do three things: to stop incoming shots on goal with various parts of her body, to clear balls safely away from the goal-cage with her feet or stick, and to play the angles when positioning herself defensively out in the circle. All of these activities require her to venture out of the cage to a distance that will cause spectators to have a cardiac episode then and there and to commit herself to tackles that appear to be foolhardy in the extreme. Good goalies play well out from the goal.

The Goalie positions herself in the "ready" stance as an attack begins to develop midfield: feet as close together as the pads allow, knees slightly bent, head up, weight forward and balanced on the balls of her feet. Both arms are bent slightly out from the sides, the left hand open and palm facing the attackers to stop any high shot, while the right hand chokes up on the stick, flat side facing forward.

As the attack develops, the Goalie follows the course of the ball, scuttling back and forth across the front of the cage, by advancing one leg to the side and then bringing the other leg up next to the first in the ready position. (Goalies have nightmares about allowing shots to go between their legs.) Meanwhile, she is feeling with stick and gloved hand for the corner posts on either side and checking on her whereabouts in relation to the penalty line seven yards in front.

The "ready" position

The double leg stop

Rather than linger inside, good Goalies advance two or three yards from the cage to meet an attacker preparing to make a shot on goal. As the accompanying illustration demonstrates, moving out from the cage face along an arc from corner post to corner post, the Goalie seeks to maximize her defensive coverage by exploiting the optimum angle she can assume vis-a-vis the attacker. At the corners the shooter has a very narrow angle toward the face of the goal. From head on, her shot has a fat pie-slice within which the ball can reach the goal. Thus the Goalie will play quite close to the corner-post if the attacker's shot approaches down that narrow corridor, but an attack from dead ahead, where the angle of attack is widest, will bring the Goalie out farthest, in order to get the widest possible coverage of that angle. The ideal is to close any angle of attack by filling it up as nearly as possible with the Goalie. This has the added advantage of blinding the shooter to her target. It all turns out to be a simple matter of plane geometry.

Or it would be, were it not for the fact that the distance the Goalie can advance from the cage is limited by the ever-present danger of the attacker's passing off to an open teammate at the last moment who can then make an unobstructed shot on goal. Fortunately, the offside rule helps the Goalie in this situation. There is a distance to be discovered by each Goalie where she has the maximum coverage of the shooting angle combined with the likeliest options for lateral movement in the event of a lay-off. She must also be tight to the corner posts on attacks there, lest a carom bounce in.

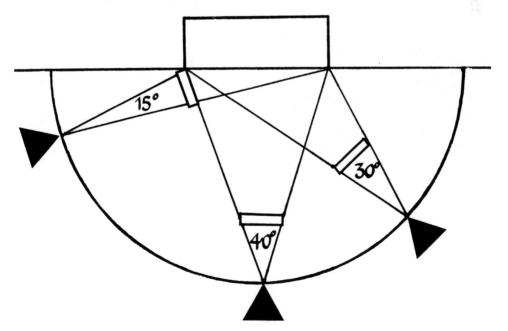

Shooting on goal angles

The premium on looking the ball in applies in spades to the Goalie, who must follow long shots on goal from outside the circle and see them pass the cage or go out of bounds. She must be alert to the possibility that an errant long shot on goal may be deflected into the cage by another attacker. Because she can never turn her back on the play, the Goalie must become adept at running sideways or backward while focusing on the ball and at performing prodigies of agility and reflex action.

Goalies stop incoming shots on goal most often with their heavily padded feet and lower legs, usually by bringing the legs together in front of the ball, stopping it, and preventing a rebound that might allow an attacker's follow-shot by literally entrapping it at her feet. She wants the ball to drop at her feet so that she can kick it out of danger, ideally to one side or the other, with one of the big square kickers she wears over her cleats. The Goalie hates to see the ball cross the open face of the cage for any reason, so that her clears are always to the side away from it — and not upfield where most of the attackers are. She must be able to kick equally well with either foot. The kick is done just like the old-fashioned football drop kick: a little hop off the free foot gives all the impulse needed for the other foot to swing into the ball and send it flying. We've seen experienced Goalies send the ball off a kick well past the midfield line.

Stop: ball at feet

Clearance kick: hop   **kick and follow-through**

Not all shots on goal require a Double Leg Stop. Weak hits can be stopped with one leg or with the side of the foot before kicking, or they may be kicked out of the way without the formality of a stop. The rapid rush of an attacker may leave the Goalie without time enough to make a two-legged stop; then she must make do with a leg, a foot, an instep, a toe — whatever's available. In all cases, of course, the Goalie keeps her eyes on the ball and knows where she is in relation to the goal face. This latter becomes important when she must try to stop a shot that is wide of her. Then she must lunge at the ball, or even execute the splits, to stop it with a leg or a stick thrust forward. In emergencies, the Goalie may execute a slide tackle on an opponent, gotten free and driving for a shot on goal, who's let the ball get too far in front of her stick. Then the Goalie slides into the ball as if it were second base, the force of her slide clearing the ball to the side. The Double Leg Slide requires the Goalie to throw the entire length of her body on the ground to block the shot of an attacker who has beaten the defender and, having gotten free with the ball on her stick, is about to shoot.

Slide tackle

Two-legged slide tackle

Hand stop: left   **right**

Slide tackles are spectacular, and sometimes leave the attacker looking like Beetle Bailey after Sarge has gotten through with him, but Goalies would rather not have to leave their feet to make a stop and clear since it takes precious moments to get back up again and ready for the next shot. She has other resources, too. Under the appropriate circumstances, the goalie can use the stick in her right hand to intercept a loose ball and pass it off to a teammate, or employ a foot for the same purpose. The stick is handy for retrieving rebounds and bringing them back within reach of a clearing kick. It is used to deflect shots on goal beyond the extended leg of a slide tackle. We've also seen determined Goalies clear with the stick while on the ground after a slide tackle. The thickly gloved left hand is free to stop high shots on goal, or the Goalie can switch stick hands and use her right glove for the same purpose. Getting back from a forward position to block a high shot on goal is never easy.

A final note: the Goalkeeper must always have a stick in hand when making a play on the ball. We've already spoken about the action that takes place around the goal on such set plays as corners and penalty shots. In game action inside the striking circle, it is the Goalie's job to direct the defense, which means that the defenders must prevent attackers from shooting on goal. They do this by marking the attackers tightly one-on-one, tackling, and making stops and interceptions. She tries to stop and clear those hits that get through into her space. Her teammates need to remember that it is not their job to screen her. All that accomplishes is to blind her to where the ball may be coming from. Similarly, clogging up the circle simply makes the Goalie's assignment more difficult, and defenders must not allow themselves to retreat or be forced back into the Goalie's space. She needs a clear area to gain reaction time, unless she decides to go for the ball in a melee. Then she loudly declares her intention, after which the defense must not get in her way. Any balls in her space belong to her. When she calls for the ball she means just that. Her teammates should not watch the Goalie during an attack; they must, however, respond to the Goalie's shouted instructions immediately. This is where talking is crucial. The Goalie's best friends are the Sweep and the Backs, who really back her up, even unto covering behind her in the cage, ready to spring out on a flanking shot on goal.

The beleaguered Goalie has one other resource available to her under attack, although it is a desperate extremity: she can always fall on the ball and cover it with her body. Unfortunately, doing that brings with it a foul call: the attackers get a penalty stroke on goal with the likelihood of scoring.

Chapter Seven
Penalties and Signals

In Franz Kafka's story, "The Penal Colony," the condemned prisoners learn the nature of their crimes only at the moment of their execution. The benighted parents of field hockey players view the whole refereeing end of the game – fouls, penalties, officials' signals – with the same bafflement. Invisible infractions are indicated by indecipherable arm movements and followed by apparently irrational penalties. Defenders perform prodigies of nip-ups and elaborate circumnavigations in front of dribbling or passing attackers to avoid violating arcane rules. Is the referee signaling a substitution or has she just wigged out?

In our wisdom, we hold that in such a high-speed game of continuous movement as field hockey, played with sticks and a hard ball, people can get hurt, and it is prudent to have rigorously enforced rules for safety. That's why, in field hockey, fouls are called for charging or body-checking an opponent, for wild or dangerous stick handling, for hitting high line-drives into crowds of players, for trying to field such shots with a stick (although the hand is okay), or for using a part of the body to stop the ball. Trying to play the ball while you're on the ground, as long as it doesn't lead to dangerous play, is permitted now. A player may not interpose her body or stick between an opponent and the ball when the opponent either has the ball or is within playing distance of it, nor may a defender cross directly between an attacker and the ball. This is, we think, a rule unique to field hockey, and the hardest for spectators to grasp who've been brought up on basketball or football.

We also believe that field hockey signals are not as clear as they might be, that referees often do not make them clearly, and that sometimes they're given so quickly that they're rarely seen by spectators wrapped up in the game. The reason for the latter is that in field hockey, unlike football, the world doesn't stop while the referee confers about an infraction with the Supreme Court, looks it up in the Encyclopedia Britannica, examines the entrails of a bird, deals a hand of Tarot, and then, after an appeal to the TV replay, makes an elaborate signal to the scorekeeper by hand and announces it on public address. Instead, the ref blows her whistle, gestures to indicate the infraction (as often as not slurring the arm movement to the point of illegibility), and then signals what is to be done with the ball, all in a fraction of a moment, so as not to interrupt the flow of this most mobile of games. We in the stands have to be quick on the uptake to follow it all, and usually it's all over by the time we, having heard the whistle, can locate the official. Maybe the hockey powers-that-be should give some consideration to the slow-eyed spectator and take a serious look at the rulebook.

However that may be, in the pages that follow we will offer definitions of the fouls, show what they actually look like when they occur, explain why they're fouls when they are fouls, and provide a description of what signals are employed to identify the fouls and to indicate the penalty each carries. We'll try to discriminate clearly between foul signals that resemble each other, as several do. We wonder why the gods of hockey don't draw up a set of signs that would be easier to read and harder to confuse.

Remember: hockey refs use whistles. When you hear a whistle, you know that something's going on — or rather, that something has just gone on, and you just missed it.

Substitution signal

SUBSTITUTION

Not all officials' signals refer to fouls, of course. One of the more common signals is that for a substitution: it consists of rotating both hands over the referee's head, as though she were grooming the front of her Mohawk. (Incidentally, all substitutes have to report to the officials' table before going in the game, just as in basketball.)

FREE HIT

The two most frequently called penalties, the free hit and the side-in, have signals that are very similar – wouldn't you just know? – but the actual infractions are different enough not to cause you much confusion. The free hit is the usual penalty awarded outside the striking circle for run-of-the-mill infractions — offside, advancing, obstruction, interference, etc., that we discuss below. The other team spots the ball where the offense occurred and gets to start their attack by hitting it. The referee's signal is to stand with one arm at her side and the other arm lifted a bit above the horizontal and to the side, the palm of the hand perpendicular and pointing in the direction up the field that the ball will be travelling when the free hit is taken. Inside the striking circle these "free-hit" fouls carry another sort of penalty called "corner," as we know.

Free hit signal

SIDE-IN

The side-in, called when one team hits the ball out of bounds (termed a side-out) and the other team gets to put it in play at the point of exit on the sideline, has a very similar signal. One arm is pointed down and a bit away from the body, the other arm pointed up and to the side, indicating the direction the ball will be travelling, as for a free hit.

TIME-OUT

A time-out is indicated when the referee crosses her arms over her head. That's hard to miss.

Side-in signal   **Time-out signal**

PENALTY STROKE

But look here: the signal for a penalty stroke is the time-out signal followed by a second signal — one arm straight up, the other pointed down towards the penalty stroke line (that foot-long line seven yards in front of the goal cage). Confusing as this signal is, it has a certain mad logic, for during the penalty shot the clock is stopped, unlike the other penalties, when it continues to run.

We need to pause here long enough to discuss this matter. A penalty stroke is a very formal, almost ritualized occasion, the field hockey equivalent of that moment in bull-fighting when the torero must go in over the waiting bull's horns and plunge his sword into the beast's heart, thereby putting himself at risk of getting a horn stuck way up into his gut. Hemingway, we think it was, called it the "moment of truth" — a phrase that certainly describes the penalty stroke. The attackers' Striker and the defenders' Goalie face each other, and the rest of the players stand back of the 25-yard line to watch. The attacker at the line can try to score with a flick, a push, or a scoop. The Goalie's feet must touch the endline, and she can't change her position once she and the Striker have told the referee that they're ready. The play starts when the referee blows her whistle. The attacker then has five seconds to make her shot for the goal, on which one step is allowed and only one push of the ball. A goal is scored when the ball goes over the end line and into the cage — the upper corner is the place to aim for, given the following limitations placed on the Goalie. She has to play with the stick in either hand, but she can't contact the ball with her stick above her shoulder, and she can't take a step or get off the end line after giving her "Ready!" cry unless as a result of the Striker's feint. The Goalie's other options – using her hands, limbs, and body to block a shot – remain in effect. The odds for and against the penalty stroke's success appear so finely balanced, the advantages and disadvantages so evenly matched, that it seems a truly suspenseful, often game-deciding, moment. Actually, for a good team, the odds are decidedly in the shooter's favor. Worse yet, if the Goalie stops the ball but breaks a rule doing it, a goal is awarded anyway. So much for Hollywood!

The question then is, what does a defending team have to do to get itself in this pickle? A penalty stroke is almost always a judgment call, since it depends on concluding that the attackers would probably have scored a goal if some foul or other had not been committed inside the striking circle: the defenders persistently or deliberately foul in the circle or on corners or keep hitting the ball over the end line. A stroke is called any time a Goalie is guilty of a flagrant obstruction, which can include covering the ball with her body. It isn't limited to the striking circle either, although that's where it's most likely to occur. A penalty stroke can be called anywhere on the field that a really flagrant foul takes place: persistent unsportsmanlike conduct on the bench or in the crowd, say, or a single outrageous incident on or off the field.

A reminder: shooting at the goal from the penalty stripe is also a method used to break ties, as we shall soon see.

Penalty stroke signal

GOAL SCORED

Another sometimes confusing signal is that given when a goal is scored, since it too is a double signal. The first sign is one arm held aloft; then the referee turns with both arms together and points horizontally towards midfield, where play will shortly be resumed with a passback as soon as the celebrations have died down. Meanwhile, the players who've just scored are jumping up and down, screaming, hugging each other, etc., as teams will do at times like this. Maybe that's the best signal. By the way, in some places the player who scores the goal carries the ball back to mid-field to re-start play. That's how we know who scored.

Goal scored signal

PENALTY CORNER

Still another signal using the referee's arms parallel, horizontal, and in front of her indicates a penalty corner off a foul in the striking circle. But this time, the arms point toward the defenders' goal. Don't forget that corners are awarded for ordinary "free-hit" fouls committed by the defense in the striking circle.

At this point we get into a series of one-armed signals that would drive even a veteran semaphore operator around the bend.

OFFSIDE

The offside signal is called only inside the 25-yard line and only against an attacker who has gotten ahead of the ball and of all but one of the defenders. Sometimes this foul will be awarded when the defense moves upfield and leaves an exposed attacker. It may not be a frame-up, but it feels like it. Another two-parter, the offside call requires the referee to point one arm straight forward in the direction that the offending attacker was going when she got ahead of everybody. Then the referee has to turn around and use an arm in the same way but in the opposite direction, to point out the direction of the free hit the other, defending, team gets. Meanwhile the other arm is firmly at her side. The ref tends to look like a clockwork soldier at times like this.

Penalty corner signal

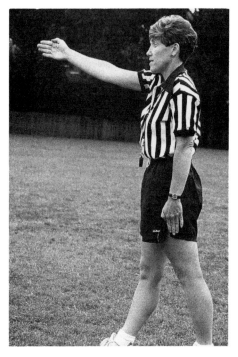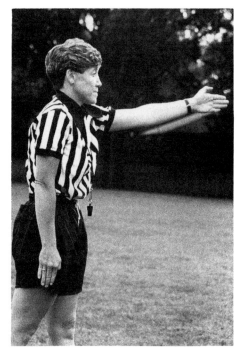

Offside signal

ADVANCING

We think that advancing is the most over-called foul on the books. It's signalled by the referee touching herself on a slightly lifted leg, knee, or foot with a hand: it looks like she's brushing a fly away. The foul itself consists of using any part of the body except the hand to strike, deflect, or stop the ball — IN A WAY THAT RESULTS IN AN ADVANTAGE FOR THE OFFENDING TEAM. Most often, advancing occurs when an attacking player's dribble or pass hits a defender's foot or lower leg and bounces off so as to be construed by the ref as giving the ball a slight advancement favorable to the defense. It can also happen to an attacking player as well, usually when a pass from behind over-runs the feet of, say, a Wing or a Link. If the ball bounces off to one side or goes on past the defender, presumably no advancement occurs, and no foul should be called, but they often are. You'll notice conscientious defenders going through a veritable gymnastic routine of hops, skips, jumps, and other gyrations to stay out of the way of a ball being played by an oncoming attacker. It's not St. Vitus's Dance: she's just trying to avoid an advancing call.

Advancing signal

Obstruction signal

OBSTRUCTION

Often you will see the referee moving one hand in front of her, round and round, as though she were winding up something invisible or stirring an imaginary bowl. Could be a neurological condition, or an uncontrollable yearning for the kitchen, we suppose, but actually it's a gesture indicating obstruction. Obstruction is a foul peculiar to field hockey, we think, and one that's very hard for American dads, who've been trained in football and basketball to screen their opponents away from the ball, to comprehend. To them, it seems unreasonable. Simply put, obstruction is what happens when a player puts her stick or body or any part thereof between the ball and an opponent who's playing or trying to play the ball. In basketball it would be called reaching in or blocking. It is usually a case of over-zealous marking. In any case, obstructing is a foul, and the victim gets a free hit or a corner, as above, depending on where on the field the infraction occurs.

Obstruction foul

THIRD PARTY OBSTRUCTION

Ever one for fine distinctions, field hockey dignifies another kind of ob-struction – third-party obstruction – with its own signal: in this case, arms are crossed on the chest and wig-wagged back and forth, so to speak, as though to get a breeze going while saying "Deary me! This won't do." The offense that prompts this odd display occurs when a player interposes herself between an opponent and the ball she wants to play in such a way as to block her out and allow a teammate the opportunity to play the ball instead. It's something like an illegal pick in basketball, but much subtler, because body-contact has usually not occurred. When you notice a player getting around an opponent by way of the Arctic Circle route, she's probably just trying to avoid a "third party," as they call it, and the free hit or corner that goes with it.

A 1993 rule change exempts an offensive player in possession of the ball and in motion from being called for obstruction, since she no longer has to "come round on the ball" before proceeding. That should open up the game a bit.

By the way, you may see the referee throw up a hand with three fingers spread out, as though she had finally gotten the bartender's attention and was asking for another round. Not so. That's just the old sign for third party obstruction that some officials persist in using. It's clear, at least.

Third part obstruction signal

Third party obstruction foul

STICK INTERFERENCE

You may see a referee trying to chop one arm off at the elbow by using her other hand as a hatchet. Don't call EMS! That's just the sign for the foul called stick interference, but better known to us old sideline types as hacking — as in basketball. Yes, yes, there's more involved here than just hacking; there's slashing, hitting, hooking, holding, and we don't know what-all vile offenses. We do know it's bad, bad, bad, and you can get called for a free hit or a corner if you're caught doing it, more's the pity. It's easy to spot, too.

DANGEROUS PLAY

Dangerous play, which can include such potentially hurtful acts as hitting a high line drive into a crowd of players (called "undercutting"), holding, making contact when marking, pushing, tripping, and charging, to name several of the most common offenses, has its own signal too. It looks like the referee is pumping an old railroad hand car very, very slowly. That is, both arms are straight out in front of her, palms down, and pointed below the waist, and she lifts and lowers them, up and down, as if she were pumping something. A free hit or corner is the penalty.

Stick interference signal

Dangerous play signal

Stick interference foul

Dangerous use of stick, "sticks," signal

"STICKS"

The signal for dangerous use of the stick, called "sticks," and meaning raising the stick up above the shoulder when playing or trying to play the ball in a manner that is dangerous or intimidating, is very expressive. The referee crooks the elbow of an arm and hooks it back over her shoulder like a sickle, as though saying, "Get thee behind me, Satan!" You'll see this called most often when a player in a crowd just hauls off with a huge back swing and tries to whack the ball into the next county with a follow-through that goes way up in the air. On a field full of running girls, indiscriminately throwing a stick up like that is dangerous: it entails a free hit or corner.

THE 16-YARD HIT

Hitting the ball over the end line is another special kind of foul that carries with it a special kind of penalty. If the attackers drive the ball over the end line, the referee will raise both arms up and out to the side, signalling that the defense gets what is called a 16-yard hit: that is, the ball is spotted opposite to the place where the ball crossed the end line and up to 16 yards from the inner edge of the end line, and the defenders' team gets to hit it up-field to restart play. (Now you know what that 16-yard hashmark is for that you saw on the diagram back in chapter two.)

16-yard hit signal

THE LONG HIT

If on the other hand a defender unintentionally hits the ball over the end line or is the last to touch it before it goes out, the attacking team gets what is called a long hit. A long hit is like a side-in with the ball spotted on the end line within five yards of the corner flag. The ref's signal for the long hit is one arm held out to the side and up at a 45-degree angle, the other arm held close to the side. She could be saying, "Thar's gold in them thar hills," but she's not.

Long hit signal

BULLY

There is also a penalty called a bully. It is called in the unlikely event that both teams commit a foul at the same instant, or the ball has gotten caught in someone's clothing (usually the Goalie's), or neither team, through some happenstance, has possession of the ball. To restart the game in such circumstances, a bully is taken at a spot no less than 16 yards from the end line – that hashmark again – and five yards from the side line — on the spot of the foul, if any. A bully is about the same thing as a face-off in ice hockey.

Bully signal

Some funny/peculiar things to remember:

- Hitting the ball with the rounded side of the stick is also a foul.
- So is tripping, using a foot or a leg to support a stick, deliberately removing required equipment or wearing or using illegal equipment, personally handling an opponent (whatever that entails), messing up on substitutions or sending in ineligible players, or stopping a ground ball with a hand.
- In restarting play with a side-in, corner, free hit, or long hit, the striker cannot hit the ball again after her first hit until another player has touched it with her stick. This rule can sometimes lead to an awkward impasse afield, as everyone stands around for a moment or two.

THE ADVANTAGE RULE (HOLDING THE WHISTLE)

Before we take up the solemn matter of misconduct on and off the field, let's discuss another unusual feature of field hockey officiating: the Advantage Rule. It is the "most important rule in the book," they tell us. It is also the least understood rule. That is so because it is the strangest rule in this or any other rulebook, since its effect is to prevent an advantage going to one side or the other as the result of its being penalized for a foul it has committed. The Advantage Rule, in short, is meant to prevent the paradoxical situation in which one profits from the punishment one receives for his crimes. (Like writing a best-seller from a prison cell.) It does so by signaling, in effect, that the referee has seen a foul being committed which she is prepared to ignore as long as, in her judgment, the penalty for it would work to the advantage of the team that committed the foul. Note well, however: the referee can later decide to whistle the foul if it turns out that no advantage would have occurred as a result of the penalty. The Advantage Rule thus also allows for very late whistles. On a more pragmatic level of discussion, it is a rule designed to keep pedantic enforcement of the rules from interrupting the swift movement of the game. A very good idea: men's sports please note — including politics and law.

If you see a referee make a sweeping horizontal arm signal, or if she raises her arm but does nothing else, she is showing you she has seen an advantage that may accrue from the commission of a foul inside the striking circle which she is going to refrain from whistling for the time being — unless of course the rule violation occurs in a dangerous or intimidating situation. In the interest of letting the game flow as it ought to do, an official may choose to ignore a foul if, say, the team that was fouled can gain or maintain possession of the ball in spite of it. A foul, in short, is not a foul when it is in the larger interests of the game's mobility to ignore it. We think that is an extraordinarily sophisticated way of viewing competition afield. A certain sort of father is sometimes outraged by this rule. We think that's another argument for it.

This rule is, surely, unique in sports. "Holding the whistle," as the advantage rule is sometimes called, is often employed when a team is on the attack and in the striking circle: ignoring fouls committed by the defense, such as crossing the end line too soon on a corner, if it means that the offense gets or retains possession of the ball in good attacking position, is allowable, nay, desirable. It is in the overall interest of the game to give the attackers an edge within the circle by keeping the game going, instead of stopping the action to call a foul. The same principle applies to the defense inside the 25-yard line, where a free hit is its greatest advantage. As the rule book says, "Only in a clear-cut instance when a defender has the ball and is in a sound position to clear or maintain possession, should the advantage rule be applied."

Field hockey is a weird game! It is also a subtle game, as whiteness the obstruction rule and the advantage rule. Understanding these two admittedly difficult concepts helps spectators empathize with field hockey referees' exceptionally demanding task. And doing that helps keep us from looking like boobs to the real cognoscenti on the sidelines.

Now, about misconduct. A flagrant foul – that is, any act which an official judges could cause bodily injury or harm to a player – is punished by the immediate disqualification of the offender.

CARDS

Field hockey is like soccer in that cards are displayed by the referee to indicate recognition of any sort of unsportsmanlike conduct, such as rough or dangerous play, abusive, insulting, or foul language, unnecessary delay of the game, entry or re-entry of an ineligible player, or any other conduct by an individual player or a team – including the coach or the fans – that the official deems to be unsportsmanlike. For the first offense, the referee displays a yellow card to warn the violator, then imposes the appropriate penalty – free hit, corner, or penalty stroke – and has the transaction recorded in the scorebook. That's called "carding" or "being carded." A second offense by the same player calls for a red card to be displayed, which means that the player is disqualified — ie, kicked out of the game. Another penalty is awarded.

Those punishments are for acts performed on the field, during play. Misconduct on the field or on the sidelines during time-out, intermission at half-time, or any other time the clock is stopped, can get carded as well and recorded in the scorebook and can lead to disqualification. If a coach is removed from the game and there is no authorized school employee to replace her, that team shall forfeit the game. (The score on a forfeiture is 1-0.)

SPECTATORS

Spectators are not immune from discipline for misconduct. They must remain behind the five-yard line drawn along the sidelines and may not stand anywhere behind the end lines. In the first instance of spectator misconduct, the referee shall suspend the game at the earliest dead-ball situation and request the appropriate coach or host site manager, depending on the affiliation of the offender, to resolve the matter. On the second offense, the game official shall suspend the game on the next dead-ball situation and award a penalty stroke to the opponents of the offending spectator's team. If the offending spectator's affiliation cannot be determined, the game is suspended until appropriate action can be taken. For a third offense the game is first suspended, as above, and then forfeited — unless local association rules mandate some other action.

GOOD SPECTATORSHIP

As long as we're on this subject, here is some advice about good spectatorship you ought to consider, bearing in mind that flagrant misbehavior on the sidelines can get you or your team into big trouble.

- Don't shout abuse at the referee: since she has all the cards, to coin a phrase, it's a dumb thing to do. If you have a question about a call, it'll save until after the game, when you can raise it with your coach, first, or one of the officials, later, in the spirit of honest inquiry. You have an obligation to be sufficiently informed about the game to raise sensible questions. We hope you don't need to be reminded that field hockey is a game for young people and not the Second Coming.
- Don't coach your child, or any other player, from the grandstand, out loud, while the game is going on: we hire coaches, who know what they're doing, to do the coaching. Your job as a spectator is to spectate, which may also include shouting encouragement and celebrating success.
- Don't abuse the opposing team, its coach, the school it represents, or its supporters: that's vulgar.
- Cheer positively. Encourage, don't carp.
- Don't lose your temper: it makes you look childish and declassé and it makes well-bred people regard you with contempt.
- Remember that the players are young people, not professionals: if you can't praise them, say nothing.
- Don't forget to have fun: the game is supposed to be entertainment.

Chapter Eight
What to do About Ties

Nature, they say, abhors a vacuum, although what that old mother has against carpet sweepers beats us. Field hockey hates tied games (or at least the people who write the rules seem to), and in consequence the rulebook has a great many "suggestions" for breaking ties, but leaves the final determination of this matter in the hands of state associations, where usually there is, as Milton put it, "chaos and dark night." It is safe to say that, from one year to the next, hardly anyone in the grandstand or on the field knows what the local procedures are for deciding tied games: they change all the time, they're rarely clear, there are too many alternatives, and nobody can remember them. Surely, we think, spectator comprehension ought to carry some weight in deciding how the game is to be played.

The rulebook offers some options — too many, if you ask us. In some local associations, ties are allowed to stand in all games except those in elimination tournaments.

Otherwise, to break a tie you can, for instance, have a ten-minute overtime period – or multiple ones – after a five-minute intermission, during which there's a coin toss (the visiting team's captain calls it) to see who gets to restart play. Teams don't change goals for overtime, they may consult their coaches during the break, there's no substitution except for injury or disqualification, and the clock is stopped after each goal is scored.

If the overtime ends in a tie, a series of penalty strokes may ensue, in which five strikers nominated by the coach from each team alternate taking flicks from the penalty stripe against the other team's Goalie. The team scoring the largest number of goals by penalty stroke wins. This latter procedure may be repeated once. If there is still no winner, the teams go into sudden-death flicks. The first team gaining more goals than the other team after an equal number of strokes, wins. There are a lot of minor rules entangled in this procedure that we're not going to go into here — that way lies madness.

Another option is to have two ten-minute overtimes followed by the flicks, as above.

A third alternative would have one – or two – sudden-death overtimes followed by sets of five one-on-ones — that is, field players from one team going against the other team's Goalie as in the penalty flicks procedure, except that here the player would dribble the ball from the 25-yard line and try to score within a ten-second time limit. Follow-up shots are allowed. Players are nominated in batches of ten by each coach. If the first five from each team don't produce a winner, the next five go sudden death.

Yet another possibility is a ten-minute sudden-death overtime period using teams with seven players on each side, counting the goalie (called seven-a-side). If no winner emerges, one of the procedures above could be used, or else – perish the thought! – the tie stands.

Then again, you may play two ten-minute sudden-death overtimes with a two-minute intermission between them. If the score is still tied, a series of alternating penalty corners in groups of three follows, interrupted by two-minute intermissions. The teams are reduced to six players a side by eliminating the goalie on offense. They alternate putting the ball in play until one team, on an equal number of corners, scores more goals than the other. Play continues until a goal is scored, the offense hits the ball over the end line, sideline, 25-yard line, or fouls, or the defense clears the ball beyond the 25-yard line. All clear?

Or, finally, you can dream up your own tie-breaker system if you can get your local association to go along with you. Something along the lines of the Chinese water torture might do.

There are other alternatives, of course. But what, we ask, is wrong with ties? There are worse things in life than kissing sisters (or brothers, as appropriate). Or if one is all THAT determined to live in a one-or-zero universe, a sudden-death overtime or two should do the job. In the case of elimination tournaments, where winners are clearly necessary, sudden-death overtimes should work. Flicks, we think, are a bad idea, from the point-of-view of ordinary humanity: that's too much pressure for school children. Any set of procedures as complicated and subject to individual variation as the present one serves only to aggrandize the mystique of the professionals in the game at the expense of the players and spectators. We can live with ties in most circumstances. Where winners and losers must be distinguished, there ought to be a single, simple, easily remembered procedure for breaking ties that will be employed everywhere.

Now then, what do you say to a little skull practice — by which we mean strategy?

Chapter Nine
Playing the Game as a Team

We could have entitled this chapter "Strategy and Tactics," thereby giving it the spurious dignity of military theory, but team play, plain and simple, is our subject here — coordinated and concerted attack and defense. Tennyson wrote it is "toil cooperant to an end" that makes sense of history and gives meaning to individual lives. It's also what undergirds successful field hockey, a game noted more for individual encounters of speed, deception, precision, quickness, endurance, decisiveness than for team play. Not heroic virtues exactly, but handier for adult life than some others we could name, and when made to work together, the basis of strategy.

With that in mind, what we offer in this chapter is a very superficial introduction to the art of field hockey as a method of systematic attack and defense. Goethe said, "We see only what we look for; we look for only what we know." Our aim is to educate your eyes, whether you're watching or playing, so that you may see the game not as a chaotic jumble of young women in motion but with insight, as a conflict between organized groups with coherent plans to achieve exact goals using power, speed, and cunning. Even so, it's well to remember, as one authority puts it, that "the game is a series of one-versus-one confrontations and the team which wins the majority of confrontations will win the game." A well-conceived and well-executed attack and defense are intended to maximize the opportunities to beat an opponent one on one, but field hockey is more a game of tactics than of strategy.

THE 5-3-2-1 CONFIGURATION

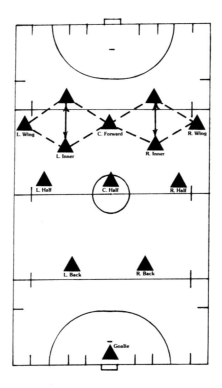

A venerable system of attack and defense, the 5-3-2-1(see diagram) has much to recommend it to players just starting out in field hockey, if for no other reason than that it offers a clear and easily understood way of distinguishing between the functions required of each player on attack, defense, and in the transition game. It's a very disciplined system with specific roles for each player, an important consideration in a game in which turnovers and sudden reversals are so frequent.

The front line of attackers consists of five Forwards, specifically a Left and Right Wing in each alley to spread out the defense and so make spaces for getting the ball centered for a shot at the goal, a Center Forward who is the point of the attack and also the pivot for passes to converging attackers on the wings, and Left and Right Inners who are positioned laterally between the Wings and the Center Forward, and – usually – lengthwise between the Forwards and the second line, the Halfbacks or Midfielders. The Inners' position as bridging elements expresses their functions on attack, since they can drop back to receive the ball from the defense and either pass it along to the Forwards or bring it through the line of Forwards as attackers themselves, attempting to link up with other Forwards to achieve a brief, local superiority in numbers inside the striking circle – 2-on-1 or 3-on-2 – that can lead to a score. In either situation, advanced or behind, they create an interlocking grid formation in the shape of an "M" or a "W" that maximizes the number of possible passing lanes and of offensive moves like diagonal, square, overlap, or through passes.

The second line, of three Halfbacks (often called Midfielders or, nowadays, Links), serves to support the Forwards' attack, control the midfield, round up loose balls and intercept clearing passes of the defense so as to feed them back to the Forwards, take the free hits, and be available for back passes from the Forwards. Because the Halfbacks form a diagonal line across the field with the outside Halfback closest to the ball the farthest up the field, they can join the attacking Forwards on the ball side, seeking to overwhelm the defense with attackers at some point inside the circle (see diagram).

The third line, the two Fullbacks or Backs, is stationed well back down the field, as its largely defensive duties require, but they play a crucial role in starting counterattacks after turnovers. Even so, the Back on the ball side of the field is upfield supporting the attack much as the Halfbacks do, while the other, Covering, Back is placed on a diagonal at her own striking circle to support the Goalie, pick up on any breakaways from upfield, and field any long hits.

Speaking generally, attackers will dribble not just to advance the ball but also to draw an opponent out of position so that a space opens up into which a pass can be sent to a teammate for a shot on goal. Similarly, moving the ball back and forth across the field seeks to exploit for a score any defensive breakdown that may occur, particularly inside the striking circle, when a numerical advantage can be achieved and held long enough for a goal. Feinting away from the ball to draw defenders out of position for a sudden thrust into the vacated area is another ploy, as is attacking in pairs.

Variations on the basic offense are many. The Center Forward, for example, can move laterally across the field at about the offside line – that is, the line of the most forwardly placed attackers – looking for through passes to get her behind the defense. Wings typically receive the outlet pass on a turnover, carry the ball downfield, and drive it across the circle in hopes that the Inners, Center, or other Wing will pick it up and score. A crossfield pass to the opposite Wing to spread the defense is an option on the way downfield. Links up close can take a back pass and then hit to the Link on the opposite side of the field, who overlaps into the attack, or she can herself overlap onto the attack, or join the front line as an additional attacker.

The game being field hockey, turnovers are frequent, and the offense can go on to defense in the twinkling of an eye. When that happens, Forwards must tackle-back or funnel – that is, crowd toward the sidelines – their opposite numbers as soon as they lose possession of the ball and thereafter continue an aggressive defense back downfield to their own 25-yard line, where the main defense of Links and Fullbacks takes charge, although the Inners may continue to tackle-back oncoming players as deep as their own circle. But the Forwards stand ready to pick up a pass from a Link or a Back on a turnover and be off to the races again.

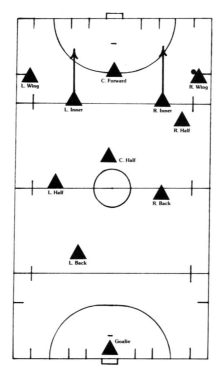

5-3-2-1 Attack:

Attack aims to draw out, spread defense, create interlocking grid of passing lanes, criss-cross field to set up 2-on-1, 3-on-2 mismatches inside striking circle.

Halfbacks and fullbacks shift toward ball side of field, form diagonal line-up, re-align as attack moves to the other side.

Forwards attack. Wings stay wide to spread defense. Inners drop back for ball, pass to Forwards, attack through front line on passes from Forwards.

Halfbacks feed the ball to the Forwards, control the midfield, intercept clears, take free hits, and sometimes join attack.

Fullbacks: upfield Back on ball side supports attack other covers inside 25 yard line.

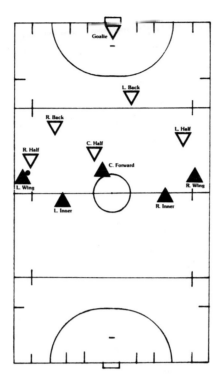

5-3-2-1 Defense: Man-to-man

In the circle, all defenders mark opponents stick-to-stick.

Midfield: Halfs mark the opponents' Wings and Forward. The backs mark the Inners. The Center Half must dominate the midefield. The Defenders stay ball side and goal side.

After turnover: The Wings tackle-back on the opponents' Wings and Halfs; the Center Forward on the Center Forward or Center Half; the Inners tackle-back oppenents' Inners or Halfs.

Links on defense mark the opponents' Forward and Wings, respectively (see diagram). In midfield play, they mark the area between their opponents and the ball unless the opponent has the ball, in which case they play man-to-man. Farther back, in the circle, Links go man-to-man on all opponents, trying to intercept or tackle to get the ball back for a pass upfield to the Forwards. The Center Half or Link is the pivotal figure on defense, since it's her job to dominate the midfield by intercepting passes and generally breaking up the opponents' attack. On many teams the Center Link also plays a very offensive position and will score as often as a Forward. Serious hockey-watchers would do well to pay attention to the Center Link: as the linch-pin of the defense and a key figure on offense, she may be the most important player on the team. She is likely be the most overlooked and under-valued player, rarely the MVP winner — unless the coach does the picking.

On defense, the Fullbacks line up against the attacking Inners, marking them man-to-man. Like the other defenders, Backs maintain a close stick-to-stick marking on their opponents inside the circle, where the going is heavy.

In a man-to-man defense, the defenders' Left Half marks the attackers' Right Wing, Center Half marks Center Forward, Right Half marks Left Wing, Right Back marks Left Inner, and Left Back marks the Right Inner. Upfield, defenders place themselves ballside and goalside of their opponents. At midfield, defenders close to the ball mark their opponents closely, while defenders farther away from the ball mark the spaces — i.e., cover. In the circle it's all tight man-to-man.

One problem with the 5-3-2-1 is that the attackers' Inners are left relatively free to move, unless the Backs can quickly jump on any of them who try for freedom of opportunity. The defensive player closest to the ball should take the 16-yard hits and free hits, and any attacker threatening to score should be marked immediately, regardless of the Covering Back.

If you take a minute to stand back and think about defending against a 5-3-2-1, it becomes apparent that a straight-up man-to-man defense may not be the best, since it is rather like trench-warfare: it encourages stalemate, eternal scuffling about in the dirt. Something that offers the defense a better chance of a turnover by pressuring the offense, while at the same time guarding against an overwhelming flanking attack on the off-ball side, might be the ticket. And so we have a defense called the "Covering Back System" (see diagram).

The "Covering Back" strategy of defense is defined by the presence of one of the Halfbacks who has dropped off to the rear and to the center on the off-ball side of the field to cover the area around the 25-yard line and protect it against an envelopment by the attackers on that side of the field. She assumes a position between the opponents' Inner, the ball, and the goal for maximum flexibility: deep enough to avoid being beaten by a through pass, but close enough to tackle an attacker who's beaten a defender. That also puts the Halfback in a situation to support either the Back defending the circle or the Half marking the opponents' Center Forward. The Covering Back thus forms the anchor of the diagonal line formed by the three Halfbacks and is the defender of the open flank. Notice that this formation allows the defense to put heavy direct pressure on the attackers closest to the ball. Furthermore, as the attacking team moves the ball across the field to attack from the other side, the diagonal of Halfbacks pivots, the ball-side Half drops back to become the new Covering Back, and the old Covering Back moves up to mark the attacker with the ball. The defensive configuration is now reversed, but the relative positions vis-a-vis attack and defense remain the same. The same basic alignment governs the players when the action moves into the striking circle: the four attackers nearest the ball are closely marked by defenders, while the Covering Back defends the space behind and to the off-ball side of them, prepared to intercept or tackle any threat from that angle. She must tackle any opponent who's beaten her defender.

There is, of course, a danger inherent in the Covering Back strategy. If the defenders don't adjust immediately to the attackers' cross-field movement of the ball, they can get caught in a square with an open lane down the middle for a straight shot into the goal with no one in the way but the Goalie. That's a shooter's dream. Or the flanking attack from the new ball-side can develop too quickly for the defense to parry, and a quick goal follows from that side.

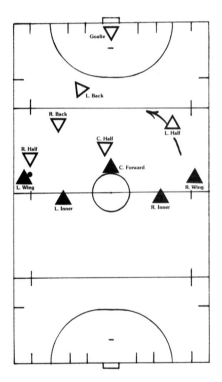

5-3-2-1 Covering back Defense:
Defense must switch sides of the field to follow swings of the ball.
The Attackers closest to the ball are marked with tight man-to-man.
Same assignments inside the circle. The Covering back tackles any unmarked attacker about to shoot. The Covering back on off-ball side covers 25-yard line area between opponents' Right Inner, ball, and goal. Alternates with Right and Left Backs on defense. Note Half and Back diagonals.

THE 4-4-2-1 CONFIGURATION

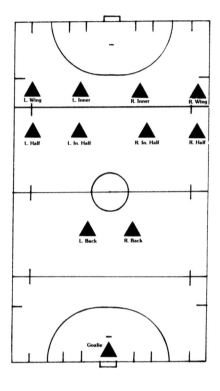

4-4-2-1 System

A 4-4-2-1 system puts on the front line four Forwards – two Wings and two Inners – and on the second line four Halfbacks – two Outsides and two Insides – plus a Left and Right Back behind them, in addition, of course, to the Goalie. While this formation costs an attacking player on the front line, it allows for seven players on defense – a numerical superiority – in the midfield, very close support on attack, one-on-one marking, and a Covering Back. Its most obvious advantage over the 5-3-2-1 is its early disruption of the opponents' attack by closing down on their Inners and denying them the freedom of movement they enjoy in the other system. This formation does cost a front line player, which means that the remaining four Forwards have a larger role to play and therefore must be fast or quick, aggressive, and imaginative on attack. For a team that has good offensive players but a defense that is suspect, the 4-4-2-1 may be worth consideration.

On attack, the 4-4-2-1 requires a lot more knowledge of the game and sophistication by the players, since it opens up the area of play and calls for much more individual player initiative. The Forwards must play the whole width of the field, for example, and are expected to do a lot of passing and cutting into empty spaces. Given such a wide-open attack, Midfielders need to be good feeders who can pass well crossfield and can join the attack by means of overlaps, throughs, and the like. Even Backs may overlap the Halfback line to start an attacking play. This is the field hockey equivalent of the basketball fast break.

On defense, the Halfbacks (Links or Midfielders) mark the four attacking Forwards closest to the ball, while the ballside Back plays a close covering position and the off-ball Back takes the Covering Back slot. In midfield play, if the ball is shot crossfield, the defending Links shift in that direction and again mark the attacking Forwards closest to the ball, the Covering Back plays close covering and the off-ball Back takes up the Covering Back spot (see diagram).

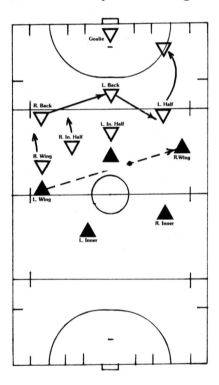

4-4-2-1 Midfield defense.

If attackers pass cross-field from Left Wing to Right Wing. Halfs shift laterally to mark opponents closest to the ball. Covering Back (Left) moves up to close cover. Off-ball Back (Right) fills the spot left by the Covering Back. (In real play, the defensive Halfbacks would be farther back and ballside of attacking Inners to help out if the ball is cross-fielded.)

Inside the defenders' 25-yard line, if a crossfield pass goes to an unmarked attacker the Covering Back marks the receiver man-to-man and the off-ball Back takes over the Covering Back's slot. In an unmarked attacker enters the attack, the closest defending Back marks her man-to-man and the other Back fills in at Covering Back.

THE 4-2-3-1-1 SYSTEM

The 4-2-3-1-1 puts four Forwards (two outside and two inside) on the front line backed up by two Midfielders or Links, then three Defenders or Backs (left, center, and right), then a Sweep, then the Goalie. The key to this formation is the two Midfielders – truly linking players – who can go forward to join the attack or go back to help out on defense. Everyone interchanges roles. In consequence, this system is noted for its balance of power on attack and quick transition to a solid, deep defense.

Another distinctive feature is the Sweeper Back or Sweep position. The Sweep is a free-ranging defensive player who is the Goalie's principal support inside the circle, intercepting through passes, tackling any threatening un-marked attacker, clearing the ball or making 16-yard hits with powerful drives to the opponent's end line, even, in desperate cases, covering behind the Goalkeeper. The Sweeper may direct her team's defense if she has the requisite comprehension of the game, since her position on the field gives her an ideal vantage point to observe what's going on. The right person at this spot can even direct her team's attack, especially if she plays well upfield. A model Sweep will combine speed and concentration with aggressiveness and savoir faire, skill at tackling, receiving, and stopping – that is to say, accomplished stickwork and dodges – and a strong, precise stroke. A consummate field hockey player, in short.

Attacking with the 4-2-3-1-1 requires the Wings to stay wide so as to spread the defense the full width of the field, and Forwards and Midfielders who can take advantage of a dispersed defense to operate together to make successful passing patterns and to free Midfielders – and even the outside Defenders – to overlap on to the attack. In this formation, the Midfielders or Links are the keys, as playmakers, directors of the ball's movement, and protectors of the ball by back-passing. Like the narrow part of an hourglass, everything passes through the Midfielders.

This truth is underlined by the 4-2-3-1-1 defensive strategy, which also depends upon the Midfielders, who must control the center of the field, keep the ball away from opponents' Inners by forcing it to the outside, and, inside the circle, mark the Inners man-to-man. The three Defenders mark the attackers' Center Forward and Wings man-to-man. As in so much of defensive field hockey, the Midfielders/Links operate in a diagonal relationship to each other, thereby offering mutual support and cover, and the line of the diagonal tilts to one side or the other as the ball moves across the field. (If you've ever played Checkers, you'll know what we mean.) The Sweeper, of course, prowls the area behind the three Defenders looking for breakaway players and loose balls.

THE 5-1-3-1-1 FORMATION

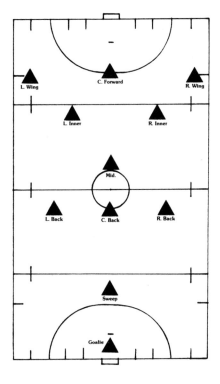

The 5-1-3-1-1 Line up

This configuration (see diagram) is based on a team with the good fortune to have five strong attacking players on the front line who like life in the circle and are adept at scoring. It also means that the two Inners must have the quickness, skills, and stamina to tackle back instantly when the ball changes hands. The Center Midfielder or Link has even greater responsibilities, and the Sweep plays like a bird of prey, ready to pounce on any attacker or ball that gets loose in the circle.

On attack the 5-1-3-1-1 tries to preoccupy the Sweeper with a very active and aggressive Center Forward who pushes the attack as deep into the defense as possible, then joins in overlap and give-and-go moves with Inners and Wings. These latter spread the defense by using the full width of the field and exploit the spaces thus created by passing combinations between themselves and with the Wings and Inners. This formation relies on attackers who are experienced, inventive, and aggressive. The Center Midfielder, who in this formation is truly a Link between Forwards and Defenders, may join the attackers on the overlap and give-and-go moves noted above, and may, if qualified, assume the role of field general or play-maker, starting the small (short) game with the Inners and Defenders and the big (long) game with the Wings and Center Forward.

Defending with this formation requires that the Wings and Center Forward back tackle and generally harass the opponents so as to keep the ball inside the opponents' 25-yard line. Meanwhile, the Inners and Center Midfielder seek to control the center of the field. To this end the Inners try to keep the ball away from the opponents' Inners by forcing it to the outside and by marking man-to-man. The three Defenders mark the attackers' Wings and Center Forward, and the Sweeper does her usual thing.

Looked at from a distance, it can be seen that the 5-1-3-1-1 is "attaque aux outrance," as the French would put it – attack to the utmost – and as such it has both strengths and weaknesses. With really confident and aggressive players in the front five, this configuration can overrun teams who're not strong on defense. At the same time, facing a more aggressive and adept defense, one not easily overwhelmed or bamboozled, the 5-1-3-1-1 can tie up the attacking Inners in their own defense and leave the three-player point of attack high and dry in the opponents' circle while a change of possession sweeps by them up the field. "Hoist on one's own petard," is the expression.

THE 3-3-3-1-1 SYSTEM

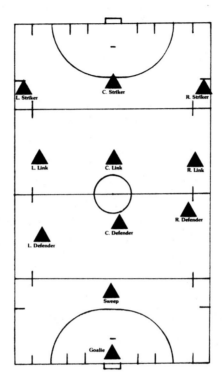

The 3-3-3-1-1 Line up

This configuration seeks to achieve the best of all possible worlds, as Pangloss remarked in Voltaire's "Candide." To do that requires a well-coached team of experienced and talented players who can take advantage of the wide-open spaces created by this most fluid and far-ranging of field hockey formations. They must be able to recognize that the spaces are there and know how to use them to maximum advantage. They must understand the game.

A look at the diagram will show that if the front line of three Strikers were to be joined in attack by the second line of three Midfielders or Links, an overwhelming force of six shooters could be concentrated against an opponent's goal. By the same token, if the three Midfielders linked up with the three Defenders and the Sweep, they would form a strong, deep defensive formation of seven players that would not be easy to penetrate. But that look would also show how important it is for every player to be a complete player, skilled at both offense and defense, capable of shifting from one to the other at an instant's notice and performing well, and operating best when playing with familiar teammates whose moves are known and whose coaching on both attack and defense has been knowledgeable and adroit. It also calls for players who are dead fit, fast, and thoroughly in control of the fundamentals of the game. And a very good playing surface helps to make this system work.

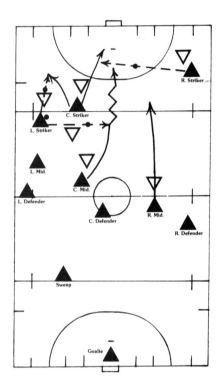

3-3-3-1-1 Attack:
Center Striker goes for the through pass. Center Link (Midfielder) goes for square pass. Left Link stays put for back pass. Right Midfielder covers.
Note the options and Midfielders' and Defenders' diagonals.

Attacking with the 3-3-3-1-1 means pushing the attack as close as possible to the opponents' goal (that's called "maintaining the highest possible offside line," in hockeyese) by advancing the Center Striker or Forward into the circle and keeping her busy hassling the opposing Defender or Sweep while waiting for a long pass down the middle of the field to tap into the goal. All three Strikers, who mutually support each other everywhere inside the opponents' 25-yard line, stay in constant motion running back and forth in lateral patterns across the field in front of or behind the Defenders, thereby posing a constant threat to execute a scoring play. Distraction is the name of this game. The Midfielders perform initially as links – hence their name – between their own deep Defenders and the attacking Strikers and also work out passing patterns among themselves to keep the ball in motion and to support the Strikers. They may overlap into the Strikers' attack themselves. So may the Defenders (usually she on the right) and the Sweep too, for that matter, who otherwise perform as before. The aim is to occupy the entire field of play and force the defense to spread itself to the breaking point.

What is characteristic of the 3-3-3-1-1 is the constant practice of players exchanging positions and responsibilities as the flow of play dictates. By using the entire field and the entire team for attack and defense, there is much more space to play with, and small games with nearby spaces and big games with wider spaces can be carried on as part of the overall attack with great facility, providing players have the technical skills – stickwork, dodging, passing – to perform a variety of moves and fill a variety of roles. Ultimately, it means that any player may properly, under given circumstances, enter the circle and shoot on goal, even Sweeps, and players should be coached to do so, even though the Strikers may be the most adept at scoring. All this suggests that 3-3-3-1-1 teams are likely to be later bloomers than other types, better in senior year and in November than earlier.

The 3-3-3-1-1 defense is built around the three Defenders marking man-to-man the opponents' Strikers, with the Center Defender or Back acting as pivot of a line that swings from one diagonal to the other as the ball goes this way or that. (The off-ball Defender covers the deep field space.) Midfielders or Links also play on the diagonal for mutual support to the end of controlling the center of the field and interdicting opponents' passes. When the ball is lost, Strikers pressure the opponents' ball carrier. Generally speaking, defence is as fluid as offence: positions are exchanged laterally as well as vertically with confidence and facility as the team moves from attack to transition to defence and back to attack again, from the forward attack to the midfield game to the defense inside the 25-yard line.

SOME GENERAL REMARKS

Let us repeat a simple truth: formations don't win or lose field hockey games; individual players beating, or getting beaten by, other individuals in one-on-one situations (called "games") do win or lose games. Done properly, attacking play seeks to maximize the length and width of the playing field so that more free space is created in which the attackers can operate with more time to see, plan, and execute ways to beat a defender or a defense by penetration and by passing, by power or deception. Finding a way to get that extra fraction of a second before firing is as important in field hockey as it is in bird hunting or skeet shooting.

In conceptualizing the game, think in terms of threes. There are three phases of the game on the field: attacking inside the opponents' 25-yard line, defending inside one's own 25-yard line, and midfield play between the 25-yard lines. There are three phases of the game's action: attack, defense, and, since this is a game of constant movement, transitional play.

A primary offensive aim is to establish a numerical superiority of attackers at a place inside the striking circle where a shot on goal can be taken to advantage. "Getting there fustest with the mostest" is what Nathan Bedford Forrest called it. The more shots on goal that can be taken, the greater the chance of a goal being scored. On average, we hear, about one goal is scored for every five shots on goal taken. (You might want to remember that statistic when you're damning a Goalie for failing to block, let us say, the ninth direct shot on goal so far taken in a game.) It stands to reason, then, that a really good defense seeks to deny attackers shots on goal by any fair means possible, of which the most obvious – and most dubious – is simply clogging up the circle with defenders.

It equally stands to reason that a good offense seeks to spread the defense as much as possible through the development of a progressive and systematic form of quick and mobile attack which, run over and over with suitable variations, will eventually cause defensive breakdowns and create empty spaces and player mismatches that lead to goals. That's what it's all about, in football and basketball as well as in hockey: running plays till they work. This spreading of the defense is not only lateral, from side to side of the field; it is also vertical, from end to end. For that reason you'll not only see dribbles and passes that zig-zag across the field, but also passes of lesser or greater length, including mighty wallops the length of the field by Sweeps and short passes back or to the side, as well as players trading positions and roles as they rotate into and out of the attack, and the like. (The rotation of players in and out of the forefront of the attack, incidentally, is also a way of conserving attackers' stamina.)

Sudden counterattacks off turnovers that drive dramatically up field for a stunning score are the natural alternates to the developing progressive attack, like the fast break in basketball or the "bomb" in football, all of which rely on surprise, speed, determination, precision, and a definite plan.

Offensive play in the striking circle is aimed at opening up lanes for drives to, and shots on the goal, deceptive over-concentration on one side or another with outlet passes to an unmarked player behind defenders for a scoring shot, or a shot taken on a rebound or deflection. Attackers typically seek to lure defenders out of the circle to the sides in hopes of getting the ball behind them and into the net with a centering pass and a hit-in or deflection. Watch for feinting moves on side-ins and free hits.

Defenders may tackle back aggressively after losing the ball, and they may also engage in delaying tactics and simple containment (or spoiling) designed to slow down or disarrange an attacking opponent in midfield. As we have seen, not every attacker needs to have a defender in her face, and field hockey makes use of many defensive ploys. Notable are: overshifting and covering (or zone defense if you will), overplaying an opponent to protect a defender's non-stick side, good old-fashioned double-teaming, poaching (a wonderfully descriptive term meaning to poke the ball away from an attacker so as to let a teammate get control of it), tackling in retreat (a kind of running harassment from the side), "directional defense" or forcing an opponent to the sideline, called funneling, and containing — that is, delaying an attacker until all the defensive pieces are in place and then clamping down, like a rear guard covering a retreat after battle. Man-to-man, zone, and a combination of the two are all defenses played in hockey. As the poet Milton put it so eloquently, "They also serve who only stand and wait, stick in hand, for something to turn up on the off-ball side of the field." Or words to that effect.

If attackers seek to create spaces in which to range, defenders seek to limit available attacking space by marking and covering, pressuring the ball carrier to misplay or to take the direction dictated by the defender. Defense should be in depth: the nearest attackers are marked man-to-man, with near cover and deep cover (zoning) farther back downfield. Defenders look out for interceptions leading to counterattack, which means that defensive support should provide the skeleton for that revolution. Lots of talking keeps communications open — as if you hadn't already noticed!

When the ball is lost way down there in the other team's circle, your team's Forwards or Strikers try to force a turnover or bad pass, prevent a penetrating pass, or deny or intercept a square or back pass. The idea is to disrupt the start of an attack as much as possible by controlling the available space. Farther back upfield, the Links (Midfielders, Halfbacks) try to control the middle of the playing field between the 25-yard lines by marking the attackers closest to the ball and covering the off-ball side. The aim is to stop a penetrating pass or dribble by maintaining a slow, deliberate withdrawal. Think of Lee after Antietam.

At the defenders' 25-yard line, the defense tightens, and in the circle all opponents are closely marked, so closely as to be unable to receive a pass or attempt a back-door manoeuvre, loose balls must be cleared to the side or upfield, overlapping Links immediately marked, and no shots on goal taken. That's how they draw it on the chalkboard, anyway.

The golden rule in field hockey defense, our sources tell us, is, "Do unto others before they do unto you," which translated means, "Always try to tackle ballside and goalside." In basic English, a defender should place herself so as to be able to intercept an opponent's pass, to keep her from making a pass or breaking around her, or to steal the ball.

Because of the inherent right-to-left bias of hockey caused by the design of the stick's face and the predominance of righthandedness in players, certain strategies become necessary. For example, defenders on the left side of the field, knowing the chances are that the attack will come on the right, want to overplay an opponent's non-stick side in order to make it difficult to handle the ball. If you can force the attacker to the side line at the same time, so much the better. Crowd her. Make it hard to get you out of her face. Tackle left-handed. Reverse-stick tackle. On the right side, defenders still want to force attackers to the outside, if only to prevent cuts to the inside and down the middle — a major boo-boo. Defenders will be even busier on this side of the field, handicapped as they are by the "handedness" (if that's a word) of their situation. Meanwhile, down the middle of the field, the upper circle is the vulnerable spot, where you have to play good "D" on both sides — "good" meaning confident but prudent. More particularly that means playing tight man-to-man marking with a wary eye cocked at places to the side or rear where zone covering may become necessary.

As if all that weren't enough, defenders are expected to play to recapture the ball and start a counterattack in the very teeth of the enemy!

Perhaps the most interesting example of this duality is to be found in the person of the Sweeper Back, who must direct the defense, play a key role in regaining possession of the ball and starting the attack, and observe – perhaps direct – the development of the attack — even join it on occasion! To handle all these roles, the Sweep must be, first and foremost, quick and fast. Sprinting is needed to "maintain a high offside line." In English that means to keep the attackers' front line as far upfield from the goal as possible. It also means being able to pick up those unmarked attackers trying to break loose on penetrating dribbles and passes like the back-door or the overlap. Or she may have to fill in for the Goalie who's off taking on an unmarked solo attacker at an advantageous angle well away from the cage. Insofar as possible, she ought to "stay home" in the middle, where her main job is, and not be lured to the periphery, unless her Covering Back is in position. Superior tackling skills are equally required in a Sweep, who must retrieve the ball and pass or dribble to start the counterattack, relying on the full repertoire of passes, from the give-and-go to the "hit for touch" — a controlled long pass. In a good 3-3-3, like as not, she'll rotate into the Forwards' attack at some point, and teammates will have to assume her position and job description for awhile. A good Sweep will know just when to do this, and do it decisively.

So we come back to a point we made earlier: in field hockey, except for the Goalie, there are no specialists.

Epilogue:
Watching the Game

Whew! We've come a long way of words, words, words since first we introduced Constance Applebee, the little lady with a whim of iron who started all this to-do about field hockey over here back in 1901.

For you spectators of hockey, the aim of our efforts has been to familiarize you with the game enough to understand generally what's going on afield, so that you can enjoy the action with some discernment and be able to discuss it with your spouse, fellow parent or spectator, or child — always supposing, of course, she's speaking to anybody this week. At least, we hope you now know why you're cheering.

For you players, we have wanted to give you an introduction to the way the game is played and to what is expected of you as a participant.

At this point, perhaps a word or two is in order that will bring all this information into focus: put simply, how do we appreciate the game as it develops during a match?

Let's start at the beginning. We hope you live in an area where field hockey is a sufficiently popular sport to be covered on the sports pages of your local newspaper with some depth and consistency. If the dailies don't, perhaps there's a suburban weekly that does. Next best, making friends with a knowledgeable veteran of the game – much more likely a she than a he – is a fast way to learn the ins and outs of the sport.

Then, when the teams line up for the opening pass-back, we hope you have a program listing the players and their positions, or at least a roster of your team, for purposes of identification. With luck you may know the names and numbers of some key players to watch out for. Take the time now to notice the formations the opposing teams are in at the opening pass-back or go into once the ball is in play: 3-3-3? 5-2-3? 4-2-3? By now you should have enough information to make these identifications and have some notion of how play may develop.

As play proceeds, keep a mental tally of the following matters:

- the condition of the playing surface.
- the score, of course, and the scorers, and who made the assist, if any.
- the number of direct shots on goal – ie, from within the striking circle or, if under NCAA rules, from within the 25-yard line – taken by each team. Are they getting the ball into the circle but are not getting shots on goal?
- the number of penalty corners, together with the result in scores. Who's setting up? who's shooting? who's stopping?
- the performance of the key players: Goalie's saves, Sweep's clears, Center Link's play making, interceptions, successful tackles, and forced turnovers, and Forwards' pass and dribble patterns and scoring.
- on attack, who's making the good passes? who's doing the good dribbling and offensive stick work? who's making the good receptions? who's making the plays? who's consistently beating her opponent one-on-one? who's making the good free hits and side-ins and corners? who's making the poor passes? who's staying busy? who's doing the assists that make the scores happen? who's muffing receptions? who's losing the ball on tackles? who's playing with the ball instead of passing it?
- on defense, who's making the tackles and getting the ball? who's the ferret who won't let go on man-to-man? who's really rushing out and marking on corners? who's forcing the turnovers and starting the counterattacks? who's there to mark a loose attacker in the circle? who's backing up the Goalie? who's consistently getting beat at one-on-one?
- which players are staying with the system, being where they're supposed to be, doing the things they're supposed to be doing? who are the loose cannons?
- which players get tired or dog it? stay cool in the circle? are fast and good stick handlers at the same time? are quick? go for the goal? are into the game? know what to do?
- who's doing the fouling? what kind of fouls predominate?
- how are the officials calling the game? closely? loosely? what are they seeing? missing?
- is the field coaching effective? are substitutions succeeding? does the coach keep her cool with players and referees? do the players seem to know what they're doing?

And so on. We could extend this list endlessly, so that it would require a staff of nine to collect and collate all the data. The secret of spectating is, as Henry James said of good novelists, being the sort of person "on whom nothing is lost." Be alert to as much as possible of what's going on afield.

Good looking! Better yet, good seeing!

A Final Note
on Further Reading

There is a considerable body of literature that has grown up over the years for the delectation of inveterate students of this interesting game. A good introduction to field hockey, if getting a bit dated, is Richard Charlesworth and David Hatt, **The Young Hockey Player** (Angus and Robertson, Sydney, Australia: 1981). Terry Podesta, **Hockey for Men and Women** (EP Publishing, Wakefield, England: 1977; rptd. 1979, 1982), fills somewhat the same purpose. Addressed to a more specialized audience but full of good things is David Whitaker, **Coaching Hockey** (Crowood Press, Swindon, England: 1986; paper 1990). Of great help to us were the three books entitled **Women's Field Hockey for Coaching Certification**, Levels 1, 2, and 3, prepared for the Canadian Women's Field Hockey Association by Kathleen Broderick and Marina van der Merwe in 1981, 1982, and 1984. Well written, profusely illustrated, and intelligently organized, these three volumes necessarily go over some of the same territory, but they are always informative. We have profited from them. Another excellent volume in the same series is **Coaching Goalkeepers**. We understand that new, revised editions of these books are being considered.

An earlier one-volume book, **Field Hockey for Teachers**, by Betty Dillahunt, Helen Riley, Maryellen Schaefer, and Harriet Stewart (Valley Farm Sports Supply, Brooklyn, Mich.; 1970), though beginning to show its age, is still worthwhile reading as an introduction to the game. The most recent annual edition of the Rulebook is indispensable: The National Federation Edition, Susan S. True, ed., (National Federation of State High School Associations, Kansas City, MO.; 1993), Susan S. True, ed. Updated editions appear annually.

The following may be found in local libraries: Rachael Heyhoe Flint, **Field Hockey**, with photos by Gordon Jones (Barron's, Woodbury, NY: 1978); Vonnie Gros, **Inside Field Hockey for Women** (Contemporary Books, Chicago, IL: 1979); Josephine Townsend Lees, **Field Hockey** (Ronald Press,

NY: 1969); and Helen T. Mackey, **Field Hockey, An International Team Sport** (Prentice-Hall, Englewood Cliffs, NJ: 1963). Books published in England, Australia, and Canada are probably most easily ordered from Field Hockey Canada at the address given in our introduction. Some equipment suppliers also list books in their catalogs.

MASTERS PRESS

DEAR VALUED CUSTOMER,

Masters Press is dedicated to bringing you timely and authoritative books for your personal and professional library. As a leading publisher of sports and fitness books, our goal is to provide you with easily accessible information on topics that interest you written by the most qualified authors. You can assist us in this endeavor by checking the box next to your particular areas of interest.

We appreciate your comments and will use the information to provide you with an expanded and more comprehensive selection of titles.

Thank you very much for taking the time to provide us with this helpful information.

Cordially,
Masters Press

Areas of interest in which you'd like to see Masters Press publish books:

☐ COACHING BOOKS
  Which sports? What level of competition?

☐ INSTRUCTIONAL/DRILL BOOKS
  Which sports? What level of competition?

☐ FITNESS/EXERCISE BOOKS
  ☐ Strength—Weight Training
  ☐ Body Building
  ☐ Other

☐ REFERENCE BOOKS
  what kinds?

☐ BOOKS ON OTHER
  Games, Hobbies
  or Activities

Are you more likely to read a book or watch a video-tape to get the sports information you are looking for?

I'm interested in the following sports as a participant:

I'm interested in the following sports as an observer:

Please feel free to offer any comments or suggestions to help us shape our publishing plan for the future.

Name _____ Age _____

Address _____

City _____ State _____ Zip _____

Daytime phone number _____

BUSINESS REPLY MAIL

FIRST CLASS MAIL   PERMIT NO. 1317   INDIANAPOLIS IN

POSTAGE WILL BE PAID BY ADDRESSEE

MASTERS PRESS

2647 WATERFRONT PKY EAST DR

INDIANAPOLIS IN   46209-1418